How to Be Kinky

A Beginner's Guide to BDSM

How to Be Kinky

A Beginner's Guide to BDSM

Morpheous

Green Candy Press

How to Be Kinky: A Beginner's Guide to BDSM

by Morpheous

ISBN-13: 978-1931160636

Published by Green Candy Press

www.greencandypress.com

Design: Ian Phillips

Printed in Canada by Transcontinental Printing Inc.

Massively distributed by P.G.W.

Contents

Foreword

I can think of no one better than Morpheous to write a BDSM book for beginners. My first contact with him was during one of his sporadic appearances in an online BDSM chatroom. He spent the better part of a year telling me to get offline and try BDSM in the real world. He wasn't looking for fresh meat or newbies to exploit. He sincerely wanted me to know the joys of experiencing BDSM in the real world. For a long time I was too scared of what I might find out there to move away from the safety of my computer, but with his encouragement and support I finally did.

When I first attended a local event and introduced myself to Morpheous in person I think he almost fell over, he was so surprised that I had actually showed up! What wasn't surprising was that he was right and getting off the computer was the best thing I ever did.

We have been friends for almost a decade and he has always been encouraging and supportive. He was so supportive that he attended a beginner's workshop put on by a local gateway group

Playing with dominance and submission is a great way to enhance your sex life.

with me even though he was far from a beginner. He brought along some other people he had been encouraging to get off the computer and try BDSM for real and he was very patient and kind to us newbies. He is as excited to share in a new Top's experience as a new bottom's.

My first BDSM experience was at a fire-play workshop. I was drawn to it but afraid too, so I asked Morpheous to hold my hand while he prepped my skin, and then gently did some fire-play (grazing passes with small torches). I'm glad I got to share that first experience with him.

Over the years I have seen Morpheous encourage many other newcomers to explore their fantasies in the real world. He preaches safety and common sense and models those behaviors in his own actions as well. He is both a teacher and a student of BDSM. His love of the dungeon is both obvious and contagious. His sense of humor is a real asset in a world where things can and do go awry. Being able to laugh at ourselves is essential when venturing into the unknown, and Morpheous isn't afraid to show his enthusiasm or to laugh at himself.

Now readers of this book will get to share this learning experience with Morpheous. He is an exceptional guide and your journey will be better for having him along.

—kharma

Chapter 1

A Look at Play

So—you've picked up this book thinking it might give you some ideas for spicing up your sex life. Maybe whips or chains or rubber outfits have at some point figured in your secret fantasies.

What are you, nuts?

Do you really want to become involved with deviants who are going to keep you out till four a.m., their beautiful bodies sheathed in tight rubber and leather; spiked heels on their feet and succulent asses proudly jutting in leather pants; chiseled chests, or breasts with pouting nipples, tightly bound with leather straps?

Maybe you have had fantasies that don't fit in with what "normal" society deems acceptable. Perhaps you have a long-standing desire to be ordered to suck and kiss the stiletto-clad feet of a beautiful Mistress while she uses you as a footstool. Maybe you long to be tied up and blindfolded while numerous hands explore every inch of your body, not knowing whose they are or where they are going next but feeling delicious in your surrender.

Or maybe you just want your hair pulled? That wild abandonment when someone is mounting you from behind, one strong hand firmly gripping your hip, the other fist wound tightly in your hair, sharply arching your head back while you both do the dance of a thousand ages across new linen with the headboard banging against the wall?

A stern headmistress can bring around the most recalcitrant submissive.

If you really want to, you can have wild sex, abandoning yourself in the arms of another person or a group of people who will set your nerves aflame, teasing and tormenting you for hours. Picture sweaty bodies pulsing with the beat in a club while some poor girl is put on display, her legs spread by chains that shackle her to a large cross and her lithe wrists pulling on thick leather restraints as other people kiss and suck her.

Abasiophilia: Sexual attraction to partners who use wheelchairs, casts, or braces. Part of Medical Play.

You can find out about a whole community of individuals who share your desires, and explore your urges with groups of people like yourself. You can discover the underground kinky toy fetish markets where you can shop for exquisite floggers, whips, restraints, dildos, strap-ons and everything in between from local artists who are kinky just like yourself.

You sure you want all that?

I know what you want. You have done all this and more in your fantasies; you have probably cruised through Internet chatrooms, or had secret personal ads put up on BDSM websites, only to take them down a little while later because you feel ashamed that there is something different about you, or scared that your deepest desires will be found out. You may have tested the waters of a fetish night without doing anything, but feeling exhilarated by the thought of controlling someone or being controlled while multitudes of kinky people surround you, watching.

I know. I was just like you.

Growing up, I always had fantasies that were well beyond what was "normal" and "acceptable" in vanilla society. They didn't interfere with my normal life—I went to school, got a job, did all the normal things that we are supposed to do. But as I got older my fantasies intensified. Vanilla sex is wonderful and satisfying but I knew there was something more to it for me, and I longed to figure out how I could find someone to share that with me, someone open-minded enough to let me tie her to a bed and tease her all night long.

It actually turned out to be pretty easy for me, and it can be that easy for you, too.

Wanting to be owned and controlled is a very common and healthy fantasy.

Research shows that BDSM fantasies and practices account for almost 20 percent of human sexuality, and those are just the people that admit to it. Let me put that in perspective: that means about one out of every four people are into the same thing you are, to a certain degree. Toss in all the other thirty-one flavors of sexuality, coupled with straight, gay, bi, lesbian and transgendered orientations, plus the many events that are being organized all the time, and there is a pretty good chance of your finding someone to play with!

This book is meant to help you figure out what you want and how to ask for it. It isn't just an instructional book on how to perform kinky acts; rather, it offers information and input from others that helps paint kinky sex with a much wider brush of human experiences than just a "top down" manual.

Abuse: When the power dynamic is non-consensual.

What Is Kinky?

What does it mean to be kinky? What is BDSM play? What goes into turning your bedroom into a den of iniquity? How do you "get kinky" on a shoestring budget but with a wickedly creative mind?

Exploring your sexuality can be a wonderfully encompassing experience. Owning your sexuality and being able to communicate what you want without shame or fear is a normal and beautiful process. However, no matter how exciting your fantasies are, please keep in mind that this book only deals with activity between consenting adults. You should never coerce someone into sexual play that he or she doesn't want, nor should you do anything to someone that isn't previously negotiated. If you feel you have fantasies that are too dangerous or involve nonconsensual situations, you should consult a professional counselor or therapist. Being kinky can be wonderful but it also comes with the responsibility for handling more charged or loaded emotional, mental and physical situations than one might normally find him or her self in.

Your sexuality is one of the most valuable aspects of life, to own, to share, to give away in a moment of passion: nothing tops the excitement and satisfaction. Learn to keep it safe and happy so that you can enjoy this next step into "postgraduate sex"!

When you first start snooping around Internet sites dedicated to fetish sexuality, or perhaps as you peruse the pages ahead, if this is the first time you have explored the topic, you will see a bunch of shorthand terms that people practicing kinky sex use to define themselves and their preferred roles. Let's start with BDSM and ease you into it all.

Aftercare: Is the time after a play session where the partners calm down, chill out and cuddle. It is a great time to be supportive and help each other come back in touch with reality.

This is an overlapping term that encompasses many things: **B**ondage and **D**iscipline, **D**ominance and **S**ubmission, **S**adism and **M**asochism. At one point in the 1980s and earlier it was all just referred to as S&M, but as interest kept growing and the scene kept evolving, along with the variety of interests and the explosion of the Internet, the concept has grown to the point where BDSM is a universal term for widely diverse forms of kinky play and sexual fetishes. Some people focus their entire interests on a particular sexual fetish.

When we pursue our kinkiest desires in a consensual and responsible manner, they can be very pleasurable for everyone involved. Some people enjoy heavy bondage, other people enjoy light teasing. Someone may become aroused by the graceful arch of a stiletto shoe with a woman's foot neatly snuggled into it, and still others might really get off on doing naughty things with chocolate sauce, bananas, and fifty feet of plastic wrap on a Friday evening when the kids have been sent over to Grandma and Grandpa's for babysitting.

Not So Fast

One of the really nice things about kinky play is that it can be sexual or *sexualized,* without the participants necessarily having sex.

Huh?

Who says that sex has to begin with foreplay and end with an orgasm? Practitioners of tantric sex focus on deep feelings of intimacy and how to keep them continually going without putting too much emphasis on the orgasm. Some people see kinky play as foreplay—foreplay that can go on for hours. Some people like this sort of play for the extreme sexual arousal that doesn't necessarily involve condoms, STD tests, or birth control. The act of dominating or submitting to someone is highly sexually charged play that gives you the freedom to creatively express yourself and explore those nooks and crannies in your psyche that house your deepest desires. The bad schoolgirl who needs a spanking after she has been caught cheating on her test by the teacher can be a

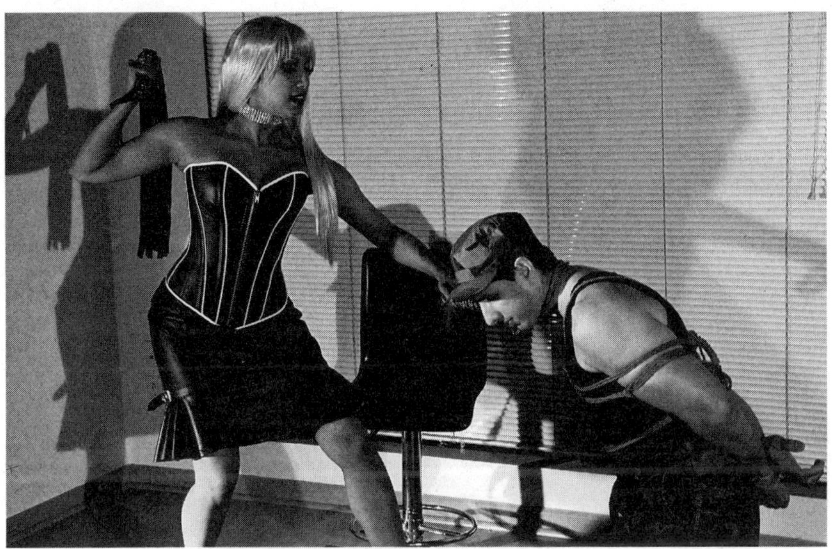

Role-play can be a way of exploring your deepest fantasies.

really hot role-playing scenario where each person gets to act out and experience a sexualized part, but *who says* the schoolgirl needs to actually be fucked in the end?

Okay, I know what you are going to say: "I say she has to get it in the end!" But let's keep an open mind here. Kinky play can create an undercurrent in your love life that ebbs and flows for days, enhancing fantasies and actual sex when you do have it. Let's break things down like this:

Say you have a regular partner and you know you are going to get laid on Saturday night, because that is what you do every Saturday night. Great! Wonderful! Both of you are going to get hot and sweaty and in the end someone is going to wind up wet, sticky, and disheveled. It can last all of ten minutes if you just want to "get the job done."

Way to go Studly McTavish!

You probably spent more time negotiating what was going on the pizza than you did planning what would be happening later in bed. Why is that? Couples get into ruts at times; how can we take mundane sex and turn it into marvelous?

Age Play: Usually referring to "Daddy's little girl" or "Teacher / student" role-play. This does not infer aspects of incest, but rather a nurturing relationship.

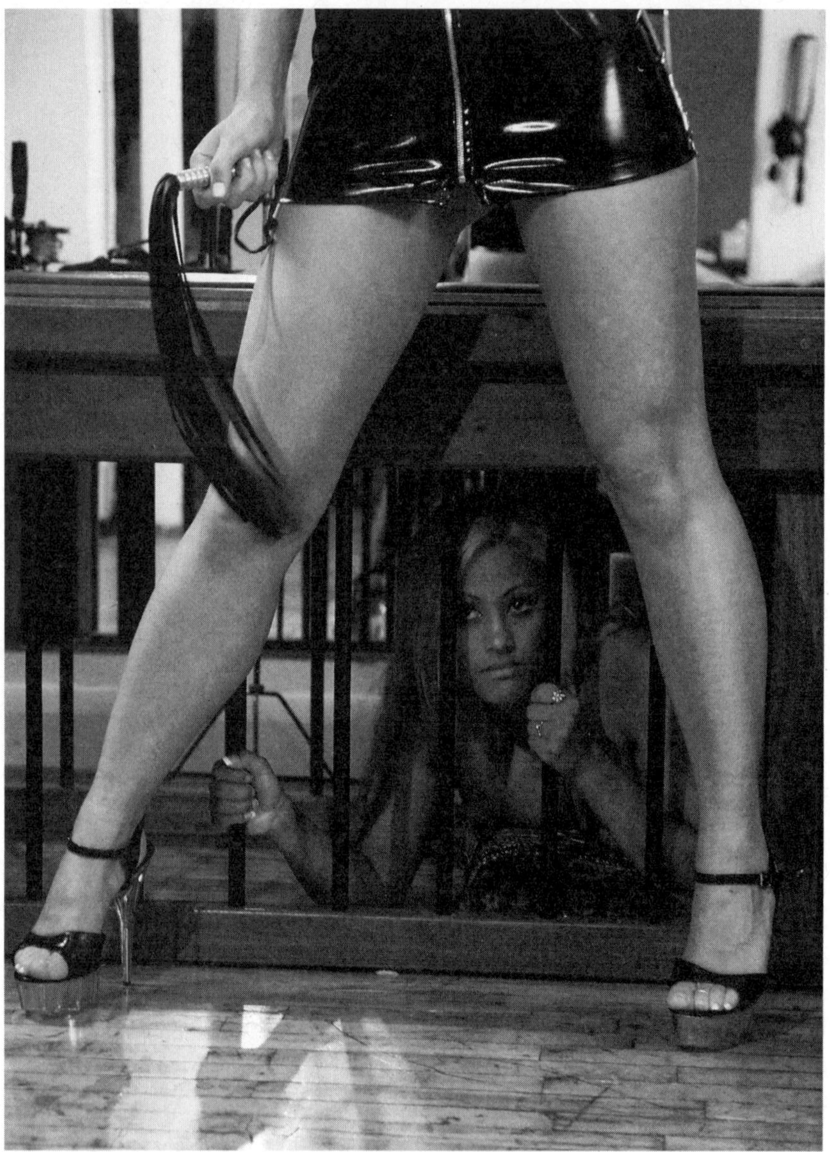

Being caged can evoke powerful emotions during playtime.

Let's reexamine this equation, assuming you have someone you really care about who also wants to be kinky. What happened to romance? What happened to teasing? I can honestly tell you that I have witnessed romance and teasing in full force in the scene, some very gallant gestures and beautiful moments of acquiescence between people who love the idea of using kink and BDSM to extend their foreplay for hours. They both know they are going to fuck at the end of the night, but why not have some fun with it? Make up some games that involve simple teasing and denial. Give your sexuality some wings and then give it room to fly. Don't let it be over in ten minutes—isn't your sexuality worth more than that?

Ankle Cuffs: Similar to wrist cuffs but designed larger to be used on a person's ankles. Typically made of leather but sometimes made of rubber, PVC or metal.

When you start to warm up the body with sexual play, endorphins—those naturally produced compounds that give a sense of well-being—are released. The sexual sensations that someone can experience after he or she has been fully warmed up are way more than if you were starting out cold. Building trust and confidence and security during playtime takes patience. Don't you want to honor the gift that your partner is giving you with more than a quick hop on and off with some nipple twisting in between?

Things That Make You Go Mmmmmmmmm

Take a look around the house and let your creative juices start flowing. What is a hairbrush for? It's used for grooming, sure, but if you turn it over can it not become a very nice percussion instrument to deliver an over-the-knee spanking to a proud, bratty girl? Ever take a good look at her silk scarves? If they are long enough, they can be a wonderful and nonthreatening way to tie up your lover for an evening.

Let's get kinky! What will you need? Hundreds of dollars for a full-latex catsuit? An exquisite collection of leather floggers? How about luscious fur-lined bondage cuffs? Mmmm...yummy.

Or you can just pick up a package of clothespins at the discount store.

Both have their merit and place. It can be a lot of fun to invest in delicious outfits and specialized toys but remember, the essence of being kinky begins in your mind. What would you do with a four-hundred-dollar flogger that you couldn't do with

Asymmetric Bondage: A way of tying someone in bondage where his body is bound in an asymmetrical pose. For example, one arm bent behind the back and other in the front. Japanese rope bondage includes asymmetrical bondage.

eight dollars' worth of chain-knotted rope? Granted, the flogger just does it with more style and flair, and fetishizing them is one of the extra-yummy things we do with our toys in the scene.

You are limited only by your imagination. Being kinky is a state of mind, not a shopping list of expensive toys to play with. Some of my favorite scenes have been head trips that lasted over hours of intense connection with someone special. It starts with having an idea of where you want to go with your playtime and partner. Personally I stay away from carefully detailed scenes; instead, I keep a few important ideas in mind that I would like to explore and that way as the scene unfolds I can let it be a fluid moment of passion rather than a scripted evening.

Developing your kinky mind requires that you tune yourself in to opportune situations. Taking control of a situation, knowing that what you are going to do will make your lover melt is where the joy in being kinky lies for me. For instance, one of my favorite scenes involves inserting a butt plug in my partner and then taking her for a ride across a particularly bumpy part of town on the back of my motorcycle.

The mindset for being kinky can be broken down into three categories:

Penetration: penetrating partners with things (if they want that)

Bondage: tying them up or otherwise restraining them

Sensation/Safety: everything under the sun that can deliver sensation: massage, feathers, prickly things, percussion; and of course Safety—lets keep at least one foot in reality shall we?

PBS for short. I'm sure you will never look at public TV the same way again.

These are the three general areas that really round out a scene. Take a little from each and you may find yourself having two Saturdays and a Sunday in your Friday night.

Setting the Stage in the Boudoir

There are lots of little things you can do to prep the bedroom so that when the time is right you already have the stage set. For instance,

Erotic rope bondage is a lot of fun and relatively easy to do.

plan ahead for a bit of restraint. As I've noted, silk or nylon scarves are wonderful—strong and soft at the same time. If you can find them long enough, you may want to tie one end around each bedpost or down on the legs of the bed. Especially if you have a bed where there is a little bit of room on the inside of the frame, they can then just be tucked between the mattress and box spring for when you need them. There will be more on knots in chapter 7.

Candelabra are wonderful and really set the mood. And, if you have six burning candles (find a low-temperature wax to start!) bathing the room in a golden light, how about taking one of them to use for hot wax play?

Most of us have heard about how you can put hooks in the ceiling for kinky play (see *Better Built Bondage Book* on securing to ceilings in Resources). Here is what is going to happen when your friends come over after you have finished installing rings in the ceiling:

Belting: Striking someone with a belt or some other narrow strap.

"So, that's an interesting place to hang a plant, right in the middle of the room."

"Yep."

(Awkward silence)

"Um, what did you want on your pizza again?"

Expect to go through this exchange. You aren't fooling anyone about why the rings are there. Hell, you might as well put the rings in the middle of the room because you can't get any decent access with a sub jammed in a corner. Just accept it and have fun with it and don't elaborate when quizzed unless they prod you for more. Silence is a powerful tool, and we don't want to involve others nonconsensually. Sure some of your friends are going to look at you funny when they notice. It is going to happen. Trust me.

How about this account of an embarrassing moment:

I was house-sitting for my folks years ago. I was in my midtwenties and full-on into expanding my kinky side. They have a wonderful farm and a big barn with an empty hayloft. I was dating two submissive girls at the time and they had both been over for an afternoon of playtime. When it came time to clean up, being the responsible and lazy Dom that I am, I stuck the strap-on harness (a full rubber one with stainless steel buckles and rings, made by Aslan Leather), the dildos, butt plugs, and a humongous double-ended dong in the dishwasher for cleaning. I turned it on…and then forgot about it. Hey, I was exhausted, the girls had just left and all I wanted to do was sleep.

The next day, I got up do more conventional house-sitting chores like mowing the lawn, and eventually my folks came home.

Here is what it sounded like:

"Hi dear, did you have a nice time while we were away?"

"Oh sure, I cut the lawn for you and just goofed off all weekend," I said as I walked through to the TV room….

Mom at this point was busy unpacking her things, and then reached for the dishwasher (which I had still forgotten all about).

When I heard the *clack* of the dishwasher lever being opened everything came rushing back but it was too late at that point;

time slowed just like in a John Woo movie. All that was missing was a white dove flapping in the background.

"OH MY GOD WHAT IS THIS???? WHAT HAVE YOU BEEN DOING, WHO HAS BEEN OVER???" I rushed into the kitchen and my mother was holding the twenty-inch-long double-ended dong, waggling it at me in a very threatening manner.

At this point my father turned on his heel and headed for the garage. He is a very smart man.

What to do? Understand that while they adored the one girl I was dating in a vanilla sense, they had no idea the other submissive and I were currently involved, and they hated her. We had been involved years earlier and she was a magnificent bad girl (my weakness) and I couldn't let them know that I had had a full-on orgy with the two of them in the barn, on the living room sofa, in the basement with them tied up to the I-beams, across the kitchen table doing things that would make the Romans blush, et cetera. I did the only thing I could do at that point. I had to draw upon my courage, look her straight in the eye, and lie to my mother.

"Er, they are mine?"

"OH MY GOD—THEY? THERE ARE MORE??" she said, dropping the double-ended dong and proceeding to yank out the racks and discover the strap-on harness, butt plugs, and a bright purple ten-inch dildo with its gracefully arched shaft ending in the head of a dolphin.

"GET IT ALL OUT OF MY DISHWASHER!!!" And she stormed off slamming doors in her wake.

Note to self: be more vigilant with dishwasher duties.

She actually went a little grayer that day. And she stopped talking to me for about a week. Which was nice, I enjoyed the silence.

So far that has been the worst-case scenario in my life of goofs. And I lived through it and most likely you will too. Do what you can and just grin when caught with the feathers in your mouth. You might be embarrassed to the maximum amount but blame it on being kinky. For god's sake don't run and hide.

Birching: Using a bundle of light thin rods, typically made of freshly cut birch switches. Similar to Caning.

1 A woman's scarf can be great for improvised bondage.

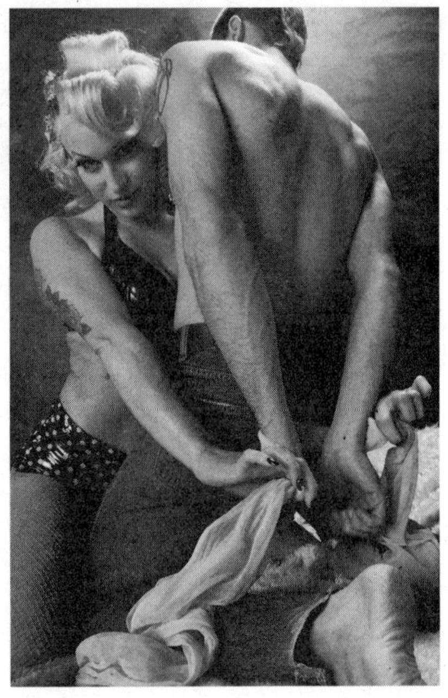

2 Start by firmly putting your partner's hands behind his back.

3 Wrap the scarf once around.

4 Cross the ends so they point up and down.

5 Bring the ends through the middle, one above and the other below.

6 Make one overhand knot in the middle between your partner's wrists.

7 Make one more knot and snug it down.

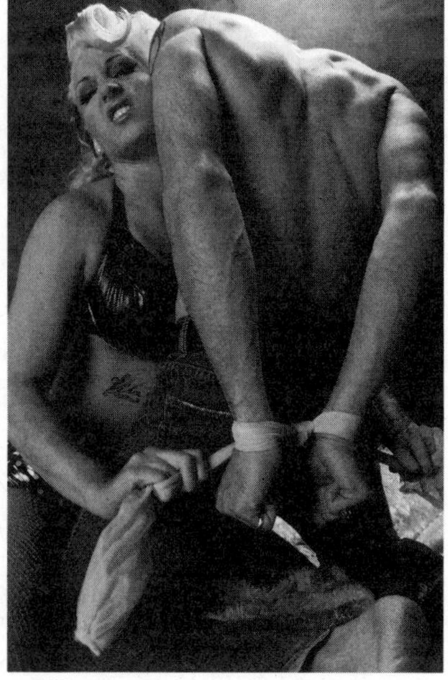

8 Enjoy!

Other suggestions for setting up your bedroom dungeon:

Throw pillows are indispensable for stacking and restacking for sex positions, especially for anal sex missionary style. Ikea sells them by the carload and they are machine washable! Take some time to make your den of iniquity welcoming and warm feeling. Check to see that your lamp isn't within swinging distance of your new flogger. Move things out of the way.

There will probably be a good amount of lube flowing around your new dungeon so look for a water soluble one that doesn't stain. Silicone or oil-based massage lubricants can sometimes stain sheets, especially white ones. Have a few of your secondary towels handy, like under the bed or off to the side. You probably don't want to use your best towels unless you really are into pampering.

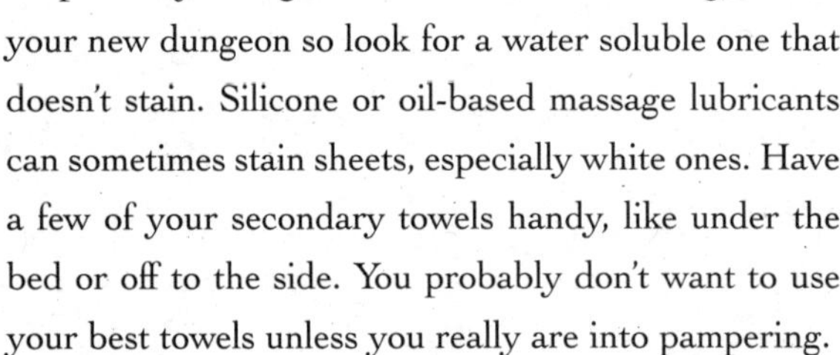

Getting Ready for a Scene

- ✔ Test your toys on yourself beforehand.
- ✔ Have ropes tied to the corners of the bed and tucked under out of sight.
- ✔ Have low-temperature candles at hand.
- ✔ Set aside towels for cleanup and a blanket for cooldown.
- ✔ Get your best and hottest outfit.

Got a jar or container for the condoms or dams?

Where are you going to keep your toys: hanging on a rack in the closet or tucked away in a drawer somewhere? When I have a partner come for a playdate, I have her do the arranging of my toys for me. I find it is a nice way to ease the sub into a play headspace and she gets to think about which way to arrange the toys and which ones she might want me to use on her (Oh, come ON, submissives, you know you have put some really yummy toy you love front and center in the lineup hoping the Dominant or Top will use it on you first!). I have my own dungeon, but in my bedroom I use my grandmother's antique hope chest she received on her wedding day. It has a beautiful walnut veneer and is deep and wide with a drawer down below that holds canes and other long instruments.

You'll want to keep things neat and presentable; who's going to want to play with a slob? If you can't take care of the barest necessities like having a clean bedroom, what does that tell your potential play partners about the care and attention you will pay to them and their safety? Dirty clothes and dirty plates in your bedroom will turn someone off immensely. Do everyone a favor and clean up—and this goes for personal hygiene as well.

Of course you don't have to be limited to the bedroom. I like to look for the opportunity to be kinky anywhere. Kitchens have lots of tasty toys one can play with. A pancake flipper makes a very mean spanking instrument for a cook who burned the cookies; an apron has long strings for tying someone's hands together while you ravish him on the counter. Hallways have nice close quarters your partner can't escape from; living rooms have couches and ottomans with legs for tying ease. You don't need massive amounts of room; your devilish mind can come up with all sorts of things even in limited spaces. I once did a small, intimate scene in an airline seat with my submissive on a flight to Montreal in which a few of her fingers were tied to each other with thread to keep her in the right mindset that she was mine and under my control. She still had her hands free for mobility; just two fingers were restrained as a reminder of what was to come when we finally got to our hotel in Old Montreal. This is a perfect example of taking advantage of an opportunity to turn an ordinary situation—in this case, a boring flight—into something that sets the stage for more excitement to come.

Chapter 2

Social Parameters

Now that you have a general idea of what goes into kinky play, let's take a look at some of the roles that are associated with it. What is a Top, bottom, Switch, Dom, sub, slave or Master and what does each do? What the hell are we talking about and why all the labels? Here is a very quick breakdown of what they are and how they dovetail with other terms or roles:

Dominant: Someone who assumes the dominant role in sex or playtime. The boss in charge. One who has a desire to control or have power over another in playtime.

Submissive: Someone who likes to be sexually submissive or passive. The receiving person from a Top or Dominant or Switch. Can also be service oriented without any overt sexual activity.

Switch: Greedy play pigs who always make a party a real happening place! These are sexual beings that can play the Top or bottom and move fluidly between the two at any given time. Make sure you always invite these people to your parties.

Ball Gag: A gag made of a rubber ball attached to a strap. The ball is fixed in the mouth with the strap fixed around and buckled behind the head.

Top: Someone who can play the dominant role when required, usually only for certain situations, regardless of his or her orientation. For example, I have a very good friend who identifies as a Master who routinely has his slave top others just for his visual enjoyment.

Renting time in a fully equipped dungeon can be a great way to explore fantasies with your partner.

Bottom: Looks like a submissive, but like the Top he or she can just be playing a role when required. Sometimes in smaller areas when there are few people to play with, all four of the kinky people in Thunder Bay, Ontario might get together as Switches and top or bottom to each other regardless of how they identify, since some playtime is better than no playtime.

Master or Mistress: Someone who identifies with a lifestyle choice to dominate someone (a slave) 24/7, in a Total Power Exchange (TPE).

Slave: Someone committed to the lifestyle of BDSM, putting his or her entire being in her Master or Mistress's care and control. This is considered an extreme form of BDSM, the flip side of the TPE.

BDSM: Overlapping terms Bondage and Discipline, Dominance and Submission, Sadism and Masochism.

There are also brats, Daddies and little girls, ponies and puppies, corporal punishment and rope sluts, naughty nurses, bad babysitters, bullies, leather bois, adult babies, cross-dressers, and more. Fetish roles and interests can be narrowed to a fine point if you so desire, but there are some general roles that most people use to help them frame their personal experiences. Keep in mind this is about kinky people and the roles they assume during playtime, and doesn't necessarily apply to your vanilla life.

You may not be able to decide where you are on the scale for labels. You don't have to label yourself immediately. Take some time to figure out what you like and how you like it. This isn't a race but rather a journey. When you first start out you may feel that defining yourself might limit your ability to take advantage of opportunities for flexibility or personal growth. Revel in the experiences you like and see how much you enjoy them. Take your time exploring hedonism and sample from all the thirty-one and more flavors of sexuality.

That being said, some people do enjoy labels.

> I choose my label, submissive, for convenience, to suit a situation, as something quick that offers a general framework until I am in negotiations, which are much more intense. I need open communication with partners, especially new ones, regarding

Blindfold: A scarf, strap or some other implement designed to cover someone's eyes to prevent them from seeing.

things they like or what I like, and what I like depends on the partner and the situation. The labels don't have to be strong definitions; what's key is seeing them as rough guidelines that give you an idea what the other person is into. Still, sometimes labels can be really hot, especially during role-play. The word *slave* has such a history and is such a loaded term that it helps put both me and my partner in the right headspace for a scene almost immediately. I even love the way it sounds when Sir drags it out, "Slaaaave"—it sends a shiver up my spine.

—gregg, submissive extraordinaire

If the Cuff Fits: Exploring Roles

When you are first starting out it pays very well to listen carefully when people talk about their role orientation. Communication is a two-way street and nurturing a dialog will give you a much better idea of how they see themselves and their interests. Individual interpretations of the basic roles in BDSM and the desires that fuel them naturally vary, but there tend to be underlying commonalities among participants. For instance, just about anyone identifying as a Dominant will be expected to be the facilitator of a scene; to be responsible and in charge of the scene, his emotions and physical reactions and those of the participants under his control; to be in charge of planning for or delegating those responsibilities; to be honorable and be willing to be accountable.

There are lots of variations on roles, depending on the individuals involved and the situation. While mining the Internet for information you have probably come across the topic of "topping from the bottom." This describes the situation where a bottom is directing a scene. This gets a bad reputation from the community when it is used in broad general terms. There are those that get enjoyment out of providing themselves as service bottoms or service Tops to those who are just learning about BDSM. People just starting out in the community often find that being students to a mentor or going to educational workshops can expedite learning the nuts and bolts of a particular dynamic in kinky sex. More experienced players who are willing can help newbies by "topping from the bottom." I like to think of BDSM play as a partnership and when it is done between two people that care about each other (even if it is only for a few hours) it is a great way for newbies to get exposure and explanations about certain activities.

Brat: A submissive or bottom who purposefully has a "difficult" persona for playtime. Usually the Top will need to apply a strong-armed application of an OTK spanking.

The possibilities for endless kinky fun can come from dressing up for each other!

Bondage: Securing someone with rope, cuffs, rubber, plastic wrap, chains or other restraints.

(Mentorship will be fully covered in chapter 9.) It can really set the stage for fun times down the road.

For example, say you just met this really hot guy and you are a newbie who really wants to learn how to top and say, just for convenience sake, he is an experienced submissive or bottom who loves having his nipples twisted. You just happen to be alone with him on a Friday night, along with a bag of clothespins from a hardware store and an eagerness to make him squeal like Ned Beatty in *Deliverance.* Because he is experienced, he knows what he likes, how he likes it, and for how long he likes it, and he can teach you that—*topping from the bottom.* This is a great way to start a Friday night date and it gives you the chance to explore how things like clothespins and nipple clamps are properly attached to the body (see photographs in the next chapter for instructions) and additional things the two of you might do.

Where "topping from the bottom" can go awry is if you have a play partner who is a bottom and he or she is only interested in having his own personal needs and interests met. This sort of individual is self-centered and only sees you as a way of having his desires fulfilled. Playtime needs to be a time where both of you can explore and have your own interests and needs met, rather than being a one-way dynamic.

> For a Dominant, it helps to know what the sub is into, so getting feedback from a new partner is essential. There is a lot of pressure in being the Top or Dominant, to keep the play or scene going, to be one step ahead of where the submissive is. Why should the Dominant hold all that responsibility? Some bottoms are very specific about what they want; they may have an interest that is narrowly defined, and I need to know so I can build the scene around that and still have my own interests served.
>
> —Electric Melissa, ass-kicking gal

But hang on there, cowgirl: before you start ruling with an iron fist, you have to be a well-balanced person who is capable of

1 Have your partner lean into you.

2 Fit the ball gag in gently, careful of his jaw.

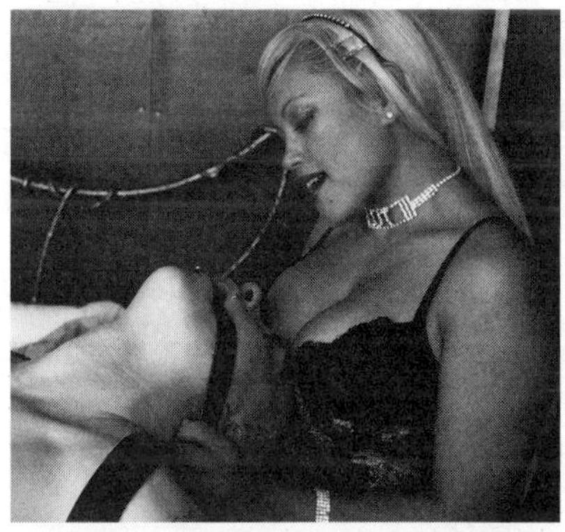

3 Bring the straps around the back of his head.

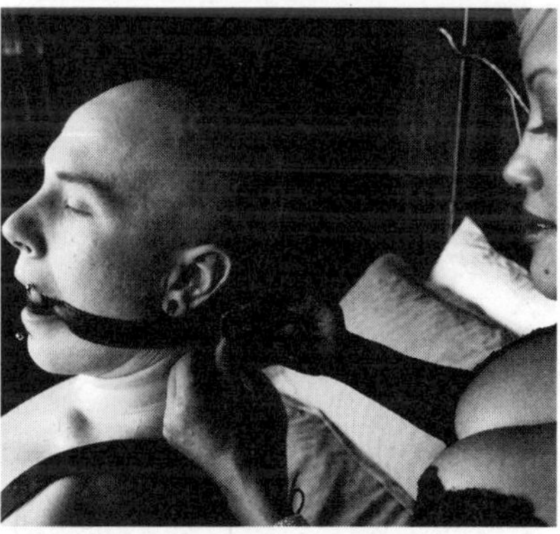

4 Draw the strap through the buckle.

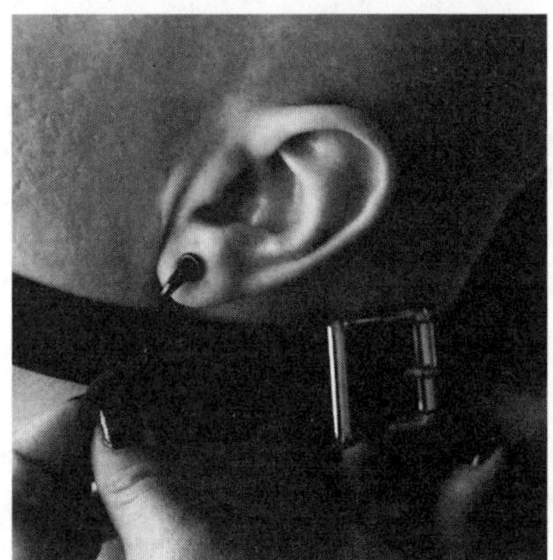

5 Set the hole that isn't too tight or too loose, you need to be able to loosen it easily.

6 If your partner is uncomfortable, he can use a safety signal such as grunting three times.

Boundaries: Established limits as to what you will or will not do. Involves "soft" and "hard" limits.

compassion and understanding. A Dominant or Top sometimes has the difficult job of having to keep one foot grounded in reality while the bottom or submissive gets to revel in the loss of control. So what do Dominants or Tops get out of being in charge when the submissives get to have all the yummy and not so yummy things applied to their nipples/toes/lips/balls/asses/minds/souls?

> I enjoy this generally, but I like it best when both the slave and I are into it in a way that doesn't feel forced. Meaning we both play our roles seriously enough but with humor and genuineness. I like it when the role-play develops naturally and well or naturally well. What turns me on is when the slave suffers gradually and almost wholly for my sake. When he pushes his limit to more than he might ordinarily be able to handle, but pushes himself to go there for me. He does it, goes through with it, mostly or fully to please me. To entertain me. I have a natural tendency to be sincerely and slavishly worshiped without fail or question. As a princess I expect to be and enjoy being pleased and entertained, as far as possible and as much of the time as possible. I love being both extremely sweet and extremely sadistic and I find it enhances my role when the slave is properly worshipful, admiring and always ready and willing to suffer whatever I *feel* like dishing out.
>
> —Princess Sadako, Domme

Power Exchange and Responsibilities: Dealing with "Drop"

Communication is vital at every stage, including in the aftermath of a scene. When you build a scene in real time and you both get hot and sweaty and then orgasm and are so exhausted you don't even argue over who gets the wet spot, it is easy to forget what should come afterward. Negotiations should always allow for time afterward to discuss how playtime went. Maybe some little triggers were tweaked, or maybe things went great. You need to be able to communicate with your partner about what you both just did.

Sometimes people can experience Top Drop or Sub Drop and become quite emotionally fragile *après* scening. It's quite common; here you are a big bad Dominant, twisting the above-mentioned nipples and making your partner squeal and writhe, watching his face contort as you apply force and your will to his engorged nipples pinched cruelly with a cheap, tawdry clothespin from the grocery store. You have that feeling of power hungrily flipping over in your belly like an electric eel, your eyes narrow as you apply a little more pressure to see just how far he can take it before backing off. You see him relax a bit and then you twist it back again and push things just a little bit further while his mouth opens in a breathless *O*. Looking deep into his eyes that are beginning to pool, you see his chest start rising quickly as he pants through the pain with you snuggling your lips up to his ear, the pink flick of your tongue riming the outer edge and whispering, "Just take a little more, do it for me, please...."

Roles and the Community

- ✔ Take time to define yourself in a role.
- ✔ Express your desires and expectations to your partner.
- ✔ Listen closely to your partner's desires and expectations.
- ✔ Know that there is a community, if you desire to access it.
- ✔ Remember: no one has the right to intrude on your private life.

I mean, what kind of person does that to another?

Well, you.

And you need to be emotionally aware of some of the feelings that might arise from this kind of play. I will let you in on a little secret. Want to hear about the hardest thing I have ever done in kinky play? Out of all of the experiences I have had there is one moment that stands out head and shoulders above the rest. Out of all the years and variety of play, of sharing moments with partners where we laugh, they cry, I laugh cruelly, they cry some more and they shiver with delight as we enjoy this lovely dance that we do between one another, there is one moment that I will never forget.

Spanking my girlfriend for the very first time.

I had met this wonderful girl on a bright summer day years ago, just before I discovered kinky play had a label; we started dating and fell for each other. We fooled around for a month or

Butt Plug: A short, flared dildo that has a wide base designed to let the sphincter securely grip it without it falling out. the wide base is important so that it doesn't disappear into the body by accident. See chapter 8 for more on bum safety.

two and had explored all kinds of fun vanilla sex together when one night she turned to me and with a wicked gleam in her eye said, "I want you to spank me, I have been a very bad girl." I was game; I loved her, she was beautiful and we shared such passion. She climbed across my lap on her cheap Ikea couch under the decorative mosquito netting with tea lights strewn about the room creating a mellow and romantic mood. I smoothed my large hand across her ass and raised it sharply and then—

Nothing.

I couldn't do it. I really wanted to, but being brought up in a society where it is unacceptable to hit women, I had all of these conflicting emotions running through me. I wanted to put aside my societal conditioning and I tried and tried to bring that hand down smartly across her writhing ass. I would smooth her butt with my hand and then bring it up again to strike and I would feel all the energy leave my arm like an electrical appliance that had just had the power cut. WTF? Here was a squirming, beautiful woman I loved who was good to go and what was this problem I was having? I felt a three-way tug of war between my emotions, my thoughts, and my physical being. She begged and squirmed, her little ass rising up like that of a kitty in heat and still—nothing from me.

It was amazing that I couldn't do it.

It wasn't until much later that I was able to reconcile myself to this being consensual, and was able to let go and spank her bottom till it was red and rosy—but I will never forget that mental hurdle that I had to jump over first.

> It is difficult for me to hurt someone I love. I have actively been in the scene for twenty years and I still have issues with wanting to hurt someone I love. It is far easier for me to be the big bad Dominant with someone I am just casually playing with. However the other side of the coin is that playing intensely with someone I am more emotionally connected with is much more satisfying for me. —Peter, Dominant

A St. Andrew's cross is a typical piece of dungeon equipment. It was named after the Christian saint who was crucified on it.

Cat-o'-nine-tails: Multitailed whip with weighted or knotted ends, traditionally used as a Naval punishment instrument.

Big Tent or Undercover Work?

I find that there are two types of people who are involved in kinky sex. Those that want to be part of a larger collective circle, known as "the community," and those who wish to keep their desires and experiences very private. The later may keep their kinky lives secret, but they may still play out their fantasies in

Cane/Caning: A thin, flexible rod, traditionally made of rattan used for striking across the ass as an implement of Victorian era punishment.

public, though you would never suspect them of it if they walked past you on the street. Sometimes a butt plug can be worn under a smooth tweed skirt while the board meeting drags on and on, but who can tell, if she keeps her composure? This kind of naughty-in-public type of play is engaged in on a much more regular basis than you might imagine. Part of the thrill of it is the threat and subsequent embarrassment of being discovered. Wearing chastity devices or rope bondage body harnesses under street clothing, or merely going out without panties, are all fun kinky things that we can do on a day-to-day basis to help keep a kinky relationship interesting and dynamic.

> I absolutely love the idea of being "found out," the knowledge that I might be discovered wearing a chastity device under my clothes in public. I know that some people may not approve of involving the public as a larger part of the scene [see nonconsensual play in chapter 8] but the difference for me is "passive audience and active audience." Do the trees in the forest mind it if people fuck under them, if it doesn't directly affect them? As long as the embarrassment is all mine if I should be discovered and I have taken every precaution against being discovered, then I feel that this is an acceptable and very pleasurable experience. I love humiliation play and the element of "danger" and this gives me an outlet for it.
>
> —Cub Dan, Top/ bottom/slave/Switch/opportunistic hedonist

The community offers you a larger resource pool to draw from. There are more and more kink-oriented events and conventions occurring across the world. Fifteen years ago, four thousand people showing up for a single evening fetish event would be unheard of, but with the growing interest in kink and with smaller events growing into larger ones, it's not unusual nowadays at all. Northbound Leather in Toronto has had such a gathering every year for the past eleven. Folsom Street Fair in San Francisco attracts 400,000 participants and voyeurs, growing

1 Get a tasty victim and a pair of leather wrist cuffs.

2 Have her present her wrist to you with the palm facing up.

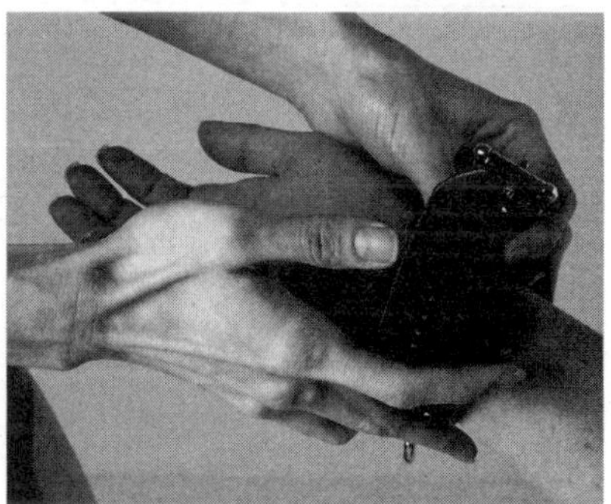

3 Wrap the cuff around it. Note: High-quality wrist cuffs will be made of high-quality leather.

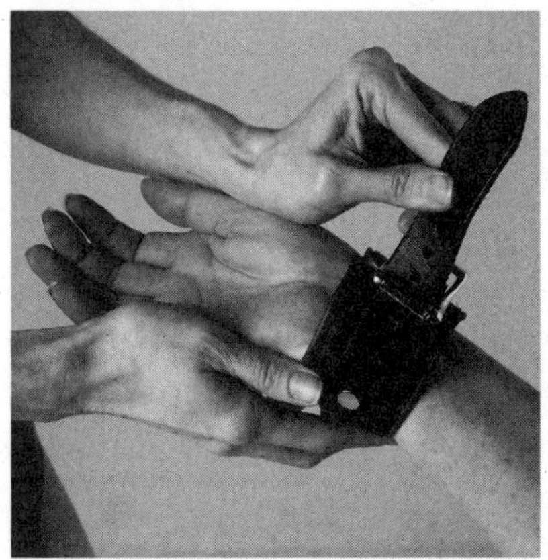

4 Firmly feed the strap through the buckle until it's firmly in place.

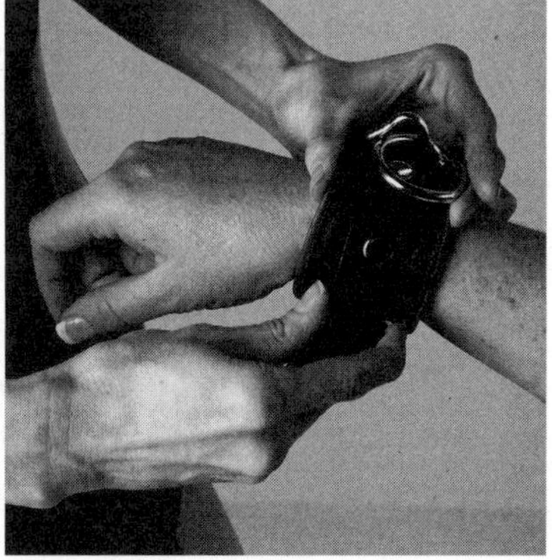

5 Straighten out the cuff and make sure it isn't pinching in any places.

Continues→

6 Buckle the cuff on the other wrist.

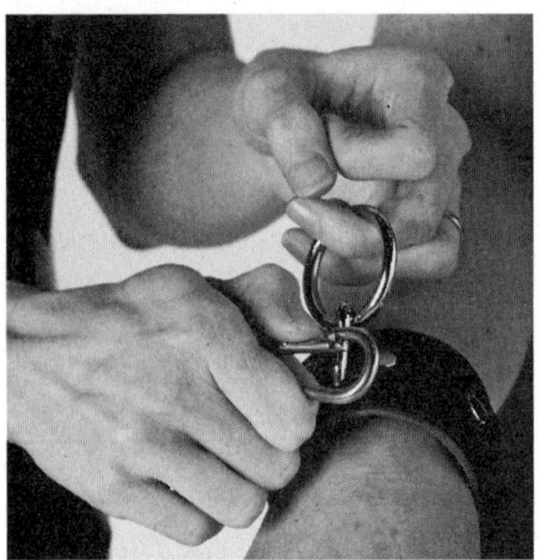

7 Take a clip and attach the rings to each other.

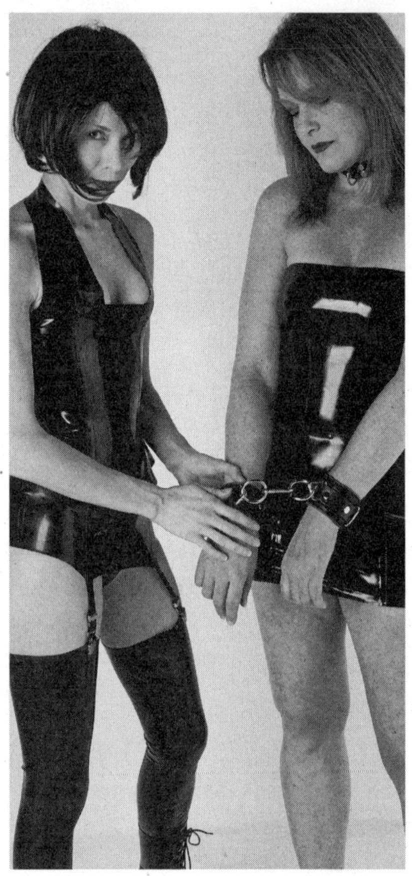

8 Enjoy your captive!

since 1984 to the point that charitable donations it generates usually top $250,000. There are full weekend conventions that have popped up all across the world that are devoted to fetishizing rope bondage or concentrating on D/s relationships; some provide a broad general overview of kinky play, others cater to vanilla people who are looking to spice things up through a mammoth sex toy show. If you have a specific interest, you are probably going to find a venue that suits your desires even if it requires a short plane ride. Human sexuality is as wide and diverse as the ocean waves.

In Canada there has been an increase in clubs that have an

even larger appeal to those of pansexual orientation. BDSM, gay, straight, lesbian, transsexual, bi, leather and femme individuals are finding homes in these pansexual clubs due to our liberal views of sex and what is legally acceptable between consenting adults.

Chastity: Preventing someone or banning him from having an orgasm or any form of genital stimulation. Some people wear a chastity belt or cock cage.

If you desire to keep your private life private for various reasons this is completely acceptable and when you run across others who are kinky they should respect your wishes. No one has the right to out anyone in any shape or form. If you choose to share your orientation with others, it is your right to do it in the time and place you desire. There are of course people who love drama, and if you would steer clear of them in any other situation, then it is a pretty good idea to steer clear of entrusting them with your sexual experiences. Even if you feel you can't find the right person to engage with, and perhaps this person offers you a chance to play when there would otherwise be none, I would urge you to reconsider. We want to be involved with people who are Safe, Sane and Consensual. Dramatists thrive on upsetting the apple cart just for the attention it brings. How do you go about finding the scene or partners if you choose to keep your private life private? This is covered in more detail in chapter 5, with a discussion of online options, but to begin with, if you currently have a sexual partner, you will probably want to attempt to "convert or pervert" him or her. Role-playing can be a great way to help open up the door for dialog between you and your partner in a nonthreatening way if you introduce it correctly. The following chapter will show you how.

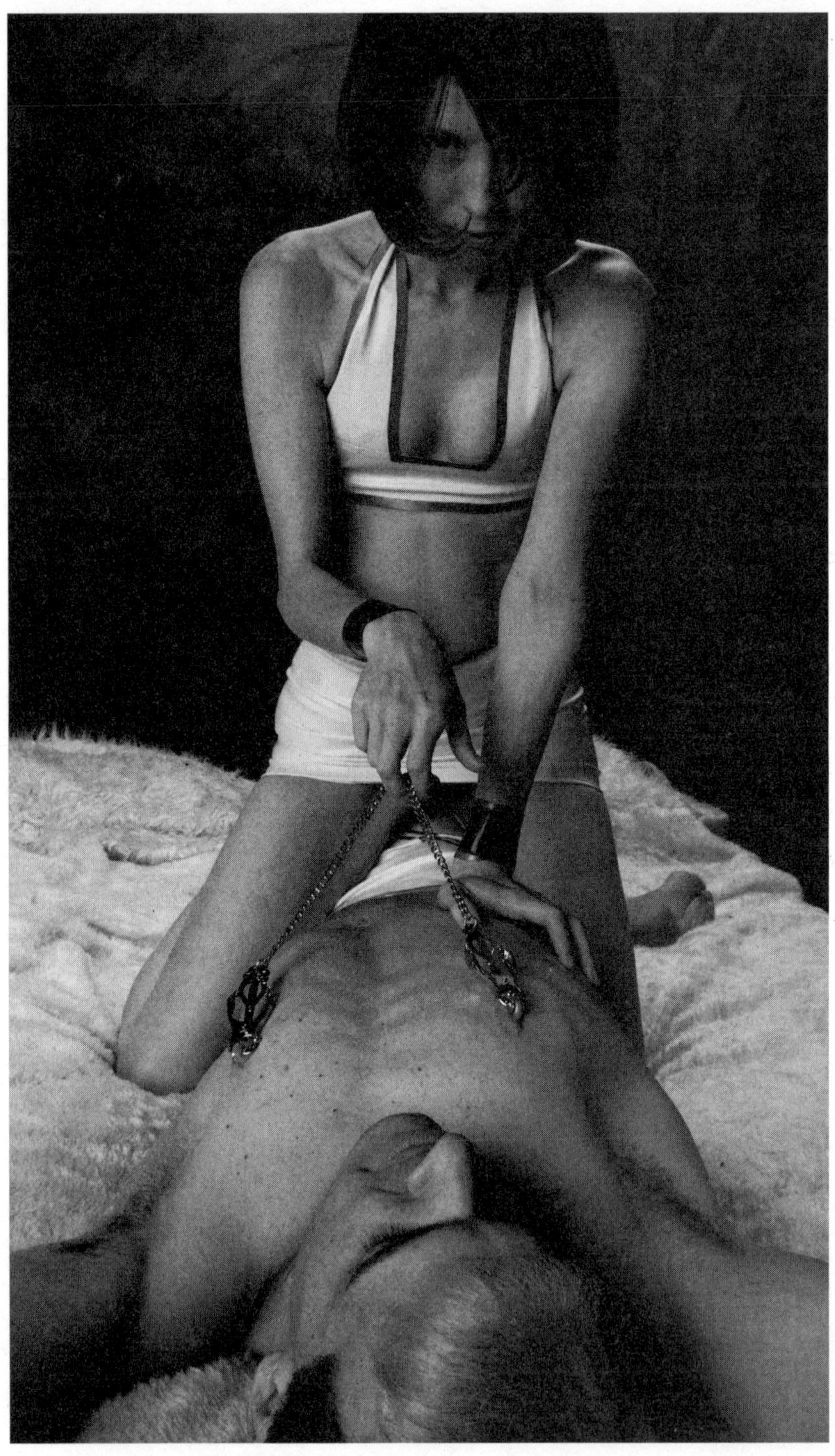

Chapter 3

Scenarios: Role-Playing, Singles, Couples and Fetish Groups

So you have this great idea about making things fun in the bedroom. You have a fantasy about taking your partner and doing all sorts of dirty, nasty and wonderfully devious things to him or her that will make her beg for more. You want to make her squirm against bonds, writhe across the bed; watch her mouth open in a breathless moan as an orgasm shudders across her skin. Perhaps you have been watching a movie where the comedic punch line is a couple all "leathered up" and you are the only one that doesn't laugh but thinks it is really hot. Where do you start? What is this whole role-playing thing about anyway? Why bother with roles?

Getting into Role-Play

Chances are you have already done some role-playing whether you know it or not. In our Western society there are gender specific roles that we adopt either wholly or in bits and pieces when the mood or situation suits us, usually in everyday life. Have you ever taken your car to the garage and noticed that when the

Chastity Piercing: A body piercing used to prevent sexual intercourse, *i.e.*, double labia rings locked together or a piercing allowing the foreskin to be pulled over the head of the penis and kept firmly in place.

mechanic explains what is wrong and points at various parts (even if you don't know what the hell they are) you feel yourself adopting a more primitive swagger or possibly grunting in agreement with him?

Or, have you ever been to a club night wearing the hottest little dress you could find, with newly done highlights in your hair, and let others buy you drinks all night in exchange for your being the gorgeous and desired one?

We all play roles—that's part of who we are as humans. Some-

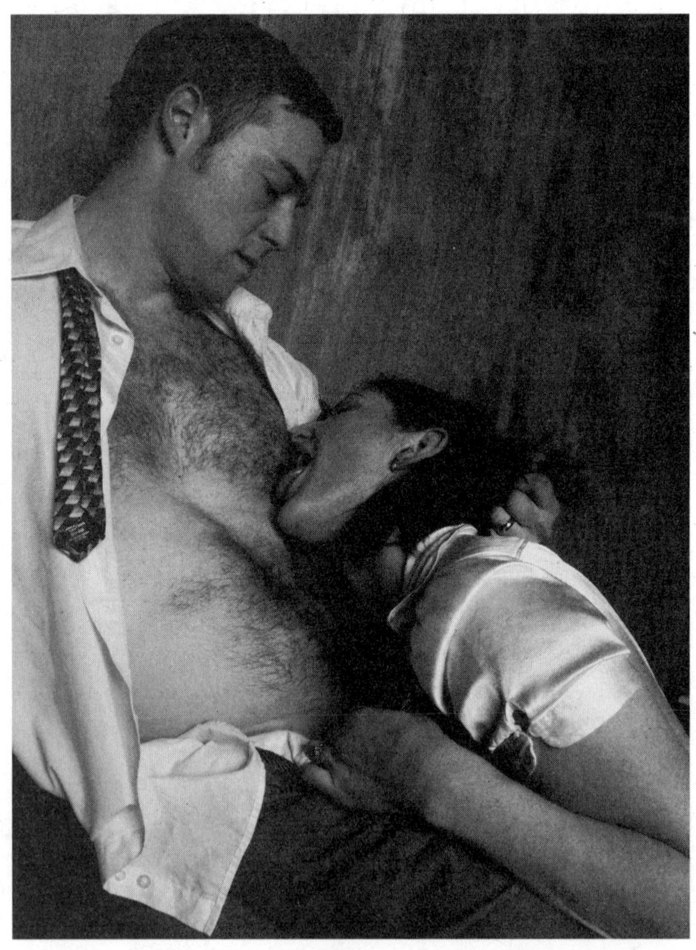

Even everyday scenarios such as "naughty secretary and her performance review" can be spicy!

Pulling someone across your lap can make her feel helpless and exposed.

times it is really hot to play with them in the bedroom as well.

Role-playing can be about adopting a persona that is different from the one we use in our everyday or *vanilla* life. In the dungeon or just when you're being sexual with a partner, it can be a lot of fun! It's a chance to escape from your normal everyday life and explore ideas and motivations. It can be cathartic and sometimes therapeutic, but we caution you not to use it as therapy without guidance from a professional. Role-playing isn't meant to be a therapeutic intervention in the bedroom or dungeon. If you want to work through a certain issue that you might have from past trauma, you need to do that with a counselor or therapist long before you bring it into the bedroom. What we are talking about here is all about consensual role-play. If you suspect that you might not be mentally stable or that you have fixations that are unhealthy, you should definitely find a professional therapist or counselor to help you.

Cinch Knot: A knot made by passing the end of a rope through an opening and around itself with a loop near the opening.

How do you get into your role without feeling self-conscious? Running around in a loincloth and swinging from the chandelier might be something that is a little beyond your comfort level to start off with. (And for those of you that it isn't—call me!) Start small, working a little role-play into your regular sex life initially. You don't have to be Tarzan, or the Gimp from *Pulp Fiction*—but what about the desperate housewife who has a leaky sink and discovers she doesn't have enough cash in her purse to pay the plumber who has been working on it all afternoon? Or, what would you do if you were a good little girl who had never before cheated on a test and then you gave in to the pressure for good grades and were just discovered by the teacher?

Roles should be believable, and yet they can be as fantastic as you like, even beyond the realm of possibility—but understand that you have to have at least one foot in reality. We can't very well have an eight-tentacled creature molesting a bunny girl without at least a bottle of lube to facilitate the action, now can we? Setting up a complex role-play scene involves the mundane tasks of making sure there are condoms or dams, and lube; that sex toys are clean and the kids are out of the house for the evening. Above all else, play should be fun, but the issue of safety should always be taken seriously. Whether in the bedroom or dungeon, everything involved in BDSM scenes should be safe.

Communication, no matter how weird the scene, is invaluable. With proper communication, creative ideas from you both will develop and assist you during the role-play scene. Communication really provides a basic foundation for those who need a boost, or a starting point for those who are lost in space. And it's a two-way street: if you expect your partner to have an open mind about your secret desire to be ravished by a firefighter, then you also have to entertain *him* when he discloses his desire to be dressed like a puppy and chasing balls down the hallway with a butt plug tail in his ass slapping across the back of his thighs. As kinky people, we need to own our sexuality and understand what makes us tick before expecting someone else to provide what we need. If you cannot communicate it effectively, how is your partner supposed to know what gets you hot and bothered?

Clover Clamp: A nipple clamp with a chain that tightens the clamp when it is pulled.

Getting into the Good Stuff

Let the scene develop from dirty talk; too much prepared script will kill the spontaneity. The fantasy should really be more of a foundation, a big pot of dirty and fun ideas that you can pull from. Dirty talk is a great way to nudge that shy partner into the beginnings of role-play. In fact, studies have shown that 58 percent of North Americans like dirty talk. It's all about making your interaction hot

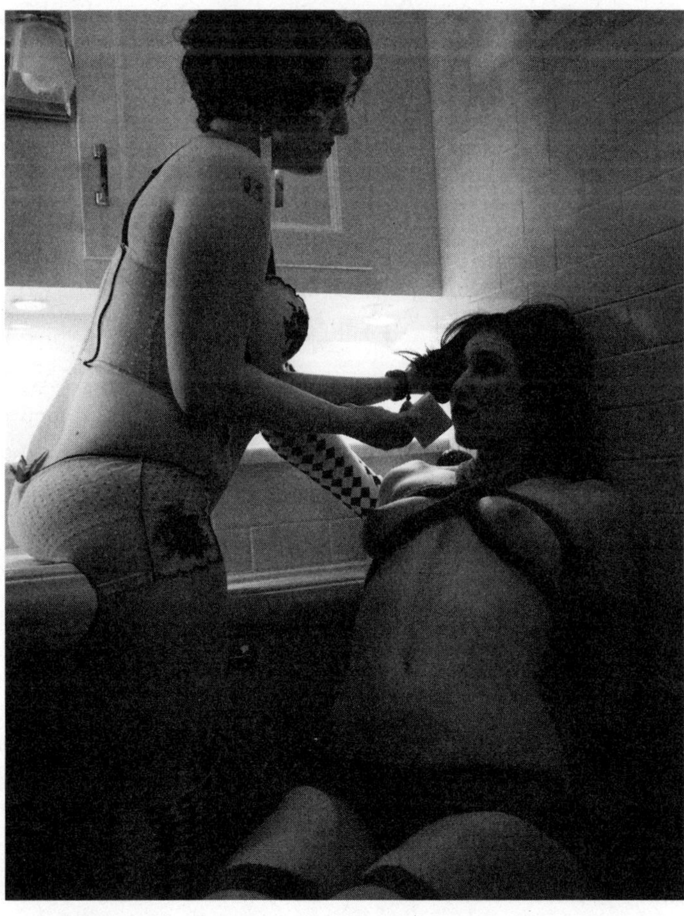

A mouthy submissive might be threatened with having her mouth washed out with soap.

and sweaty and seductive. Remember, you have to start this when your partner is all hot and bothered. You can't go from first gear to fourth right out of the gate. Get some purring going on. As with blues singing, start with a call-and-response method:

"You like that, don't you?"

"Do you like it when I bite you there?"

"Mmm... You love it when I tease you like that, don't you?"

Try two different things on him and ask him which he likes better or how he reacts differently to them. For instance: try two different floggers that are weighted differently and have a different type of leather; one might be heavy and "thuddy" and the other might be sharp and "stingy." You can try framing your question to include the role-play to add to the ambience: "Mr. Clinton, now that I have you tied up here in this lovely oval office, if I am going to take the fall for you, you are going to do exactly what I say for the next hour. Otherwise your usually understanding wife is going to get a dry cleaning bill from me. Understand? Now, I am going to hit you with two different types of floggers and you will tell me how you like or dislike each one.... Chin up, no slouching now!" I'm sure you get the gist of where this is going. (Getting back to safety, use care when playing with lit cigars.)

Role-Play Scenes

- ✔ Set up a scenario in advance with a phone call *e.g.*, a nurse has been caught molesting her patient and now is being brought before the hospital administration for punishment.
- ✔ Dress in business attire and use your necktie as a great prop for quick bondage on a bad, bad secretary who's made one too many typos.

This requires input from your partner. What you don't want is to launch into a scene with a scared little bunny who is too shy to say what she likes or wants. If you have a new partner or one that is new to this sort of play and doesn't know what he does or doesn't like just yet, this is a perfect way to bring him into a comfort zone of answering questions and engage him in an interaction.

Once you get her in the mood and begging for more you can get into second and third gear:

"Who is Daddy's little tramp?"

"I'll teach you to cheat on that term paper—you are going to stay after class and do everything I tell you to!"

Finally, once they are taking all the dirty talk you are throwing at them, you can break out the big guns:

"I am going to consume/own/mark/devour you!"

"You are going to do everything I say you will, aren't you?"

Cock Ring: A ring made of rubber or metal, or even a strap that is secured around the base of the penis. This ring allows blood to flow in but restricts it flowing out helping to keep it erect. It is important that it not be worn for prolonged periods of time.

Real-Life Examples

Big Bears

One of the roles I like to play is with bigger men—big, burly bears that are way bigger than me and I want to trick them into submitting to me through seduction. My personal fantasy is to get a tough guy to admit he wants to be dominated by me. Through my role as the Dominant I convince them that letting me play with them would be the best thing in the world to expand their sexual horizons. For me it isn't about adopting a thematic role like that of firefighter or good cop/bad cop. It goes beyond that type of role. I enjoy the role of the Dominant who is seducing the larger man to get him to relinquish his control, to create a safe space for him to explore being submissive to me. A place that he knows no one will know about. The big bears that I play with want to know that I know that discretion is important and regardless of whether they are Dom or sub or Top or bottom in the leather scene, if they come to me to explore being submissive, they know they are completely safe. What I love most about it is taking such a large man (I'm five-eight and really buff) and wrapping him in my rope, capturing him in my web, having him under my complete control. —Dart, Mr. Black Eagle 2007

The Catholic Thing

Growing up Catholic has added fuel to my kink life. Understand that French-Canadian Catholics are huge on protocol. You have to dress your best, follow all the rules, and it all blends and blurs into your real-life imprinting when growing up. My favorite role-play fantasy is one of being a Catholic Priest. As a woman

Collaring: Ceremony when a Dom and submissive symbolically commit to each other.

just the initial fucking with gender roles gets me hot and bothered and when I add religion on top of that, it makes it even steamier! The concept of sin buried within ritual—the priest being prim and proper and the word of god, yet really being the kinkiest and most deviant of them all; of setting up that role as god's personal provider, where flagellations or a hair shirt are necessary for redemption... Forgiveness of your sins that requires suffering spills into my fantasy role-playing all the time. Sometimes it is situation specific. I love the role of catching the naughty altar boy doing something bad—after all, you never know when a priest could show up in the school yard or in the rectory. Maybe I catch him masturbating in the confessional or even worse masturbating with other boys! Punishing him for his own good makes me wet. Maybe I fuck him in the ass for redemption, or make him wear uncomfortable items such as CBT [cock and ball torment] or foot binding, and there is definitely hot wax play—have to put all those candles to good use! Endurance for penance, being the vehicle of their redemption is what is centrally important to my role-play. As a Domme I have always held that my personal pleasure with the strap-on is necessary for any boy I play with, and adding the gender reversal makes it even more perverse with the Catholic situation.

—Mercury Kittie, Domme

Daddy's Little Girl

For me it is the Daddy and little girl fantasy. Older men always made me hot, long before I was collared, even when I was dating vanilla men. When Daddy and I were playing on our first date and he was holding me by the neck and he had me tied up, I asked, "Can I call you Papa?" Somehow "Master" or "My Liege" didn't work; it didn't fit at all but Papa felt right at that moment. At that point I think he said, "You can call me Santa Claus if you want, just don't stop." I loved it that he was taking advantage of me and I wanted him to. Later on I adopted the Daddy's little girl identity out of the gay culture roles around

Leather Daddy—it is not about incestuous relationship, but more about nurturing, mentoring, and creating a safe place. Even if he is twisting my nipples or torturing my pussy it is about a caring role that fosters growth. I am proudly a slave to him now and that is a constant role in our lives, unless we actively negotiate it differently for a particular situation. We have performance reviews where we evaluate each other on where we are and where we want to go. When we were first dating it was a role we would go into when we were together, but now that we are 24/7, my central identity is that of the little girl. —Lulu, Daddy's little girl

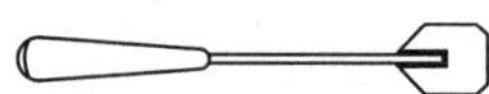

Role-Play Scenes

- ✔ Let your partner be that slutty hooker who just jumped into your minivan when you were at a red light and is now all over you.
- ✔ Pretend you are a Daddy taking your little girl on a shopping spree on which she gets pouty because you say she has to earn her purchases.
- ✔ Have your partner lay out all of the toys for the evening, taking his or her time to arrange each and every one exactly the way you desire.

Learning to Be a Lady

I see role-play as dramatic ritual where I assume a persona that can be a cathartic experience for someone that I am playing with. It gives me an ego trip that is unlike any other. I personally enjoy being the "governess" that is helping a cross-dresser realize his dream of becoming a good little girl and becoming part of my stable of girls that are highly feminized and manipulated as I desire them to be in body shape and mind. As a professional Domme I have a lot of cross-dressers who come to me desiring a safe space to explore gender reversal. I tell them that they have no choice in the matter; that they must do as I say in order for them to be complete and utterly enslaved to me. This creates an environment in which they don't have to wrestle with their desires to be cross-dressed; they can drop their vanilla lives at the doorstep and let their inner girls come forward for some pampering and firm training. Sometimes I can spend a whole session just on teaching a new little girl how to walk in heels. Occasionally I will intersperse an age-play scenario with a cross-dressing session—say, that of a new girl just entering

Consent: Approval or permission freely given in a context for someone to engage in a particular activity without coercion. Informed consent is consent freely given beforehand and being fully aware of the conditions and consequences of the activity. Consent is key in BDSM, See the previous entry on "Abuse" to distinguish it.

puberty and growing up who needs to learn how to become a lady, how to have her makeup and hair done properly, and the correct way to sit. I have a cross-dressing area in my dungeon, complete with makeup and wigs and clothing that ranges from "little miss prim and proper" to "complete slut." What I find most interesting about these clients is that some of them lead very hypermasculine roles in their vanilla lives and it seems they come to me in order to balance themselves by letting their feminine sides have a chance to breathe and explore.

—Lady Fiona, professional Domme

Kidnapped Girl

This is role-play started as dirty talk in bed when my girl was masturbating and eventually grew into a real-life experience that both of us really enjoyed. Its appeal for me is greatly based on socially taboo situations, outside the realm of what is acceptable. I kidnap a girl and force her into this lifestyle, forcing her to bend to my will and become my slave. It is all psychologically arousing for me. That is my particular edge—I can get aroused just by thinking about it. Taking her and reshaping her, forcing her into the role of my personal doll: it touches the psyche more than my cock. Luckily I am blessed with my own special woman in my life that had the same fantasy and wanted to explore it as well. I would talk about it for months in bed and then when the opportunity presented itself I took advantage of it. One weekend we were in Montreal at the big fetish ball and we both decided this would be a perfect opportunity to explore our fantasy in a whole different city and situation that could make it more believable. Our agreement was that once she put the mask on she became my fantasy for the night. She would talk to me like I was her kidnapper, I would grab her and drag her into the washroom and make her stand there when I took a piss. Or I might leave her alone with someone else and tell her that she needs to watch out, the last two girls I left with this person were never found again. It was a really amazing head-

Would you like to come and play?

space to be in as it went on all evening. It is emotionally hard to go through that for six hours, but very arousing. We did fuck that night and I took pictures of her and told her I would send them to her family (edging into her blackmail fantasies). But after the hood came off the role ended and we were exhausted and falling asleep in each other's arms.

—RetroDeviant, psychological sadist,
owner and operator of "doll"

Speed Bumps

So what happens when things go awry? How do you stumble through after triggering some hidden emotion in someone and reassure him that things are okay and you really aren't going to tie him to the train tracks? What happens if you have hit some long-buried issue that causes your partner emotional trauma?

Corset: An article of clothing which is tightly laced around the midsection, designed to lift the breasts and narrow the waist. Oftentimes made of silk, leather or PVC and including strips of rigid "boning," – higher quality corsets will have steel boning and lower quality will have plastic.

You are probably going to feel like a complete and utter shit. And you are going to blame yourself. This is because you are a compassionate person who cares about his or her partner. But what you feel and what you do are the key elements that are going to separate you from the trash out there. You are going to recognize that your partner is having a problem or issue and slow the fuck down. If he or she is ramping up in a bad way and going in the wrong direction fast you need to be his anchor, his brake, his grounding in reality. (See chapter 8 for a full discussion of safety issues and detecting genuine signs of panic.)

If you are the Dominant, it is your DUTY to ensure that your partner is safe and cared for in ALL aspects while he or she is under your control. If you are the submissive or bottom or even a play toy you are entitled to a safe environment. As Dom, you need to be able to step away from the role-playing if there is trouble and immediately become a warm and compassionate partner. This doesn't mean that playtime has ended. Your playmate may only need a little calm reassurance that everything is okay and then you can drop back into the scene. Scenes are a failsafe way of determining what is an actual problem and requires attention verses a "play" problem. For example "No no, don't do that to me!" might be a very hot way of using words in role-play that doesn't mean what it really sounds like. If there was a real problem such as the wrists cuffs being too tight and cutting off circulation, someone would use the code words that wouldn't normally tumble out of her mouth. The universal words in the kinky world have become *Green* ("Oh, I love what you are doing!"), *Yellow* ("Something isn't right…") and *Red* ("Stop, I need to get back to the real world right now!"). There are still some groups and play parties that will have house safewords that you have to honor if you are at their particular event. However with the wide variety of play parties that are available, it could be confusing to have to remember five or six different safewords. Having a universal standard of Green, Yellow, and Red works very well when immediacy in a situation is of paramount importance. I recommend that new parties starting out adopt these code words. They are easy to remember (just like a traffic light) and short, easy to pronounce words. When a submissive or bottom says "Red," that is your signal, if you're the Top, to get her some water, hug her, ask her what you can do to make her more comfortable. You need to be a compassionate partner right now, instead of "Blackbeard, scourge of the ocean blue." You can always revisit things down the road. Never ever berate someone for using his or her safeword.

Singles

You've owned your sexuality, you're hot and bothered, and you're dying to find someone to play with. How do you do that? Back in the day, before the Internet, you had to find meetings of like-minded people—meetings known, then and now, as *munches*.

Good girls go to heaven, but bad girls go anywhere they want.

Cross-Dressing: Dressing in clothing usually worn by the opposite sex.

These are casual and informal meetings that take place in restaurants or bars where there is no play at all. These are meant to provide a meeting place for like-minded people who come to share ideas, network, and converse about BDSM in a safe environment. Nowadays you can log into a chatroom, have your pick of Doms, subs, slaves or bottoms, slap that online Velcro collar on them and be off on as much as you like. Which do you think is more satisfying?

Online can be great. In my experience, since I came to BDSM before the Internet explosion, I have seen what is good about pre- and post-Internet. Formerly, if you wanted to learn a particular skill, you had to find someone who was not only an expert in it but also willing to teach you. This requires social skills and learning how to be gracious in accepting that information, plus using it responsibly in future situations. The biggest drawback of the Internet is that it can offer an illusion of expertise. There is information that used to take years to acquire and absorb, now only a mouse click away. Imagine that you meet someone who sounds like he or she knows what she's doing. She answers all the questions you pose, and then once you are all tied up she confesses that she learned everything about bondage from watching porn videos! Not a situation any bottoms or submissives want to find themselves in. Conversely, many of the older generation who went through the slow, real-life approach are reluctant to spill all their carefully gathered information, especially on the Internet where their information might end up in the hands of people who aren't as conscious of safety and carefully gathered knowledge. I am taking a chance myself! In this book you are finding out more about this great big world of BDSM and I am spilling my secrets to help bring more knowledge to people who are just starting out. Some of this information could be used in a nonconsensual situation, but my hope in writing this book is that newbies will be alerted to the signs that not all new partners are what they seem to be.

Which way are you going to go: Methodical apprentice to a master rope artist? Or cyberslut who absorbs everything he can and jumps from one fetish to another figuring out what makes him tick?

I propose a healthy blend of the two. The Internet provides a good resource for starting people down the path. I have found over the past few years that new people who come to me for play or training already have a strong idea of what the foundation of BDSM is about because of the Internet. Foundation is the key concept

Cuckoldry: When a Dom/me takes another sexual partner other than the submissive for the purpose of humiliating the submissive.

Don't be afraid to be a little saucy!

Dacryphilia: Sexual arousal in either partner by seeing tears in the other.

here. They use it as a starting place—a place to begin from. The BDSM community is highly adaptable and very good at taking care of its own. You will find that word travels very quickly and your reputation as you get involved in the real-world parties is your ticket to everywhere or nowhere. If you come to the scene and demonstrate the ability to follow the protocols, be gracious and generally have good manners, and can accompany it all with a smile and a compassionate attitude, the world will blossom for you. As people get to know you and like you, they will include you. Most likely you will start with a munch or two, then move on to a fetish night at a local club in a major city. After that, if you are good and positive and become well known for what you do or what you endure then the private parties will open up to you.

You might meet someone online and really like his or her vibe, and like what he's saying. I'm sure you have snooped around the Internet long before you bought this book and already know that when moving into a real-life meeting, you should always set it up for a public place and have a safe call in place. (See the section in chapter 8 on safe calls.) This can be an exciting time for both of you, wanting your hopes and desires to be returned in kind. Sometimes that vibe isn't there in person and no one can be faulted for that. Before you go to meet anyone, you need to both agree that that might happen and if it does you should both part on friendly terms, because chances are you are going to run into each other at the fetish club next month and wouldn't you rather have this person talk about you in glowing terms as "someone who is really great and has a lot to offer the community, but we didn't quite click," rather than saying "Stay away from that psycho!"? Honesty and integrity never go out of style.

Couples

So what if you both want to try some role-play or just some play and each of your desires and wishes don't quite mesh with what the other has in mind? Say you really want to do a long cross-dressing session where you are strapped down and your nipples are tortured, but your partner is leaning more toward putting you in the stocks and spanking your bad little ass red and raw? Negotiate and communicate with each other.

> During the early part of the twentieth century, academics such as Mary Parker Follett developed ideas suggesting that agreement often can be reached if parties look not at their stated positions but rather at their underlying interests and requirements. During the 1960s, Gerard I. Nierenberg recognized the role of negotiation in resolving disputes in personal, business and international relations. He states that the philosophies of the negotiators determine the direction a negotiation takes. His *Everybody Wins* philosophy assures that all parties benefit from the negotiation process which also produces more successful outcomes than the adversarial "winner takes all" approach. —wikipedia

DM or PM: Dungeon Monitor/Play Monitor—an experienced person who volunteers to supervise the interactions between couples during time in the event's play space to ensure safety.

Dom/me: Man or woman who takes control.

This is a situation where both parties can win. You might arrive at a nice compromise where you get some cross-dressing in along with having your ass spanked, your nipples clamped, and your upper torso locked in the stocks. Of course you may have to agree to some strap-on play or other activities that your Dom desires, but having the opportunity to look at what both of you want and need, you should be able to arrive at a nice middle ground. (For a fuller discussion of negotiating a scene, see the following chapter.)

But what happens if the play dynamic is going to include other people? There has been a lot of discussion over the past several years regarding polyamorous relationships. Some people are naturally wired as poly, preferring multiple partners to a monogamous relationship. Some people enjoy monogamy with a little flexibility to include a selected third person. Still others enjoy several mutually satisfying play relationships while nurturing a primary relationship with one particular person. Being emotionally monogamous with one person but physically poly with others is a situation that requires a lot of trust, commitment and

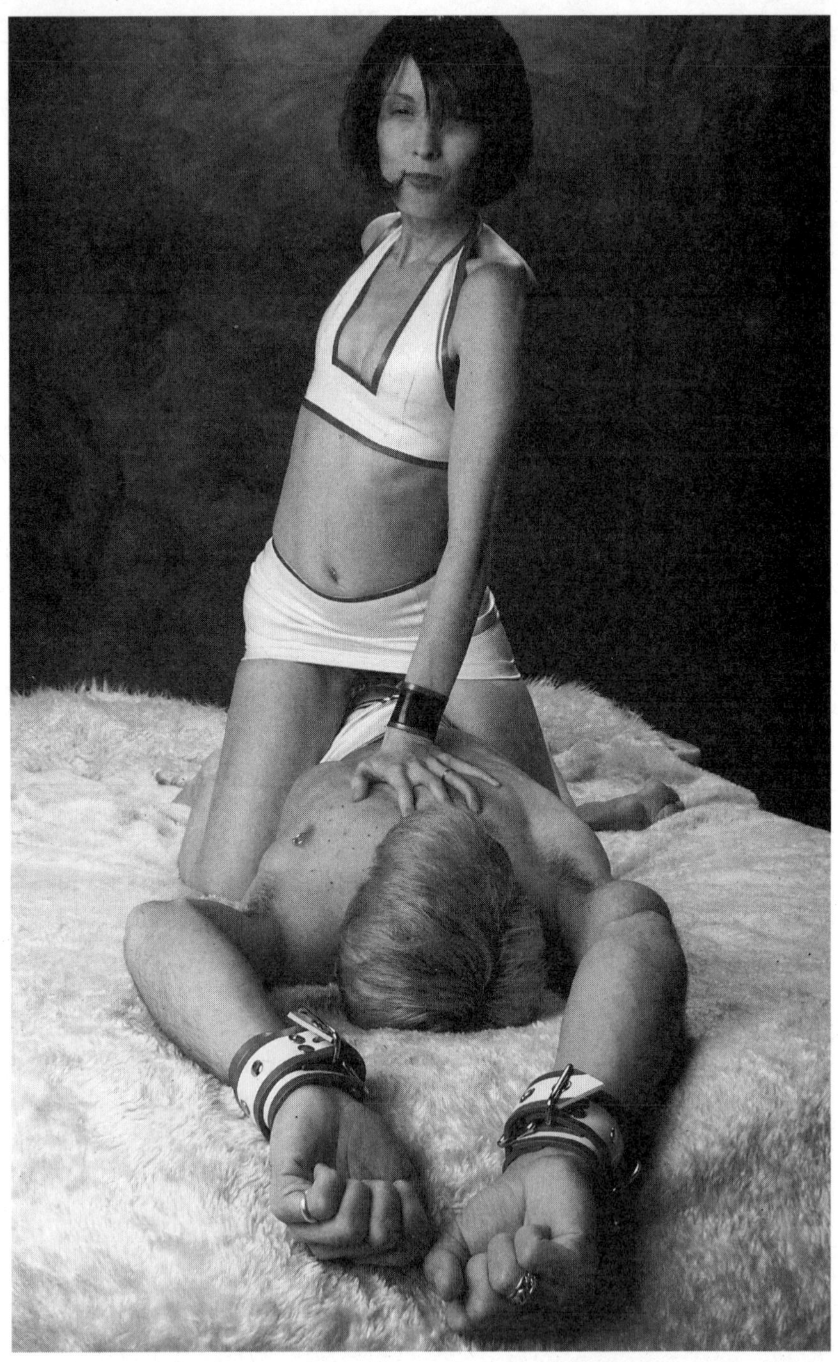

1 Straddle your submissive seductively.

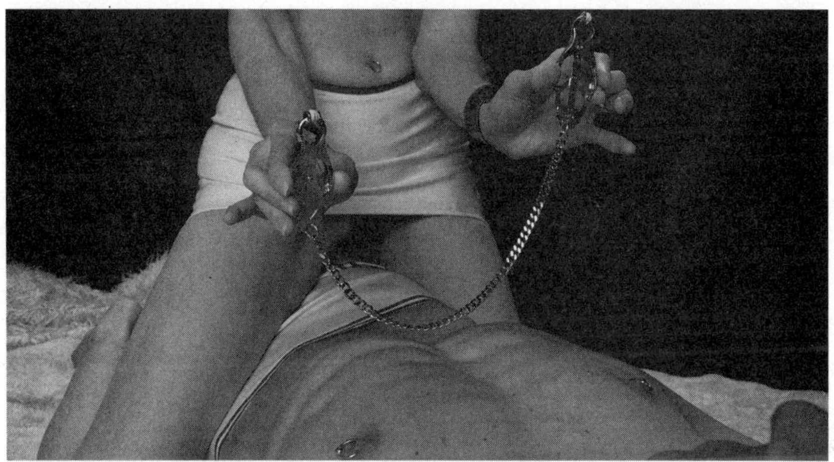

2 Squeeze the nipple clamp open (be careful not to have lubed up, slippery fingers).

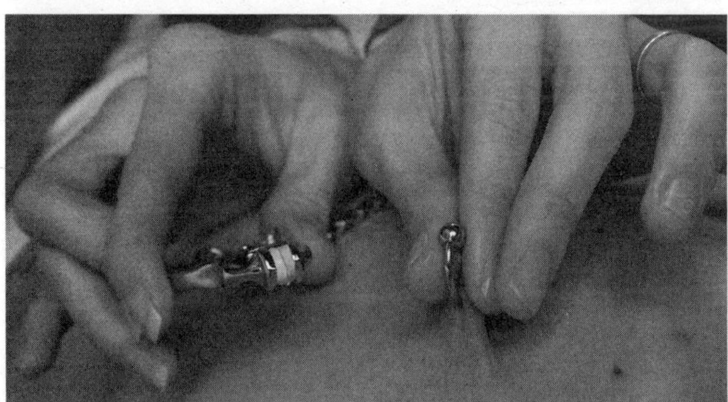

3 Pinch the nipple gently and pull it up.

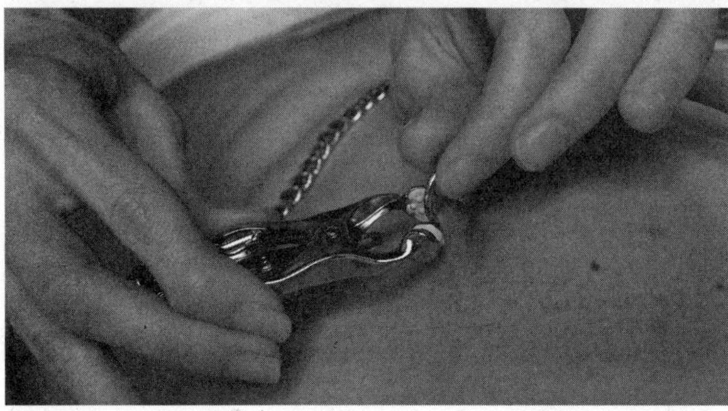

4 Place the jaws of the clamp to pinch behind the actual nipple. Continues→

5 Have them take a deep breath in and release the jaws slowly on their breath out.

6 Give them a moment to get used to it.

communication. It will force you to be completely open about whom you are seeing, what they mean to you, and what you are going to do with them. For my wife and me this represents the ideal situation. Lady Rachel and I are both emotionally monogamous with each other but choose to experience play relationships with several other people. She does so through her work as a professional Dominant; I do so as lifestyle Dominant. We find that if there is ever a stumbling point it is because one or the other is

7 When they are ready place the other clamp on the other nipple.

8 Try gently tugging and swaying the chain at first and see how they like it.

withholding. It isn't for everyone, but it seems to be very close to ideal for what we desire from our relationship. You need to talk with your partner in a safe environment and on neutral ground about where you want to go with her and what role you need her to play so that she—or he—can make up her own mind if she can or wants to go there with you, what boundaries need to be set, and what you are both comfortable with. Communicate, communicate, communicate!

Fetish Parties

Dragon's Tongue: An unusual type of percussion toy, consisting of a handle with a lash made of a wide piece of suede wrapped around it and then tapering to a point at the striking end. Creates a very loud and distinct sound and sensation when used on a submissive's back or ass.

Oh the fun we have when newbies come to their first Fet party! The wide-eyed expression, sometimes hiding behind the shoulder of the person who brought them there; other times their wild sides are unleashed and you can't even get them down from the bar/stage/stripper pole where they're dancing! Fetish parties are one of the reasons we love BDSM—the chance to dress up, get out and act sexual with others. The eye candy is hot, and the play is even hotter. Imagine yourself being led up a set of dark stairs at a downtown club you have never been to. You hear music thumping above your head, conversations, people laughing, and when you round the corner you are greeted by lights, smoke, and hundreds of people sheathed in latex, leather, feathers, fur, and maybe someone wearing a pair of black PVC boots with nothing else but a smile on! After all the years of longing to do this, you are overwhelmed at so many like-minded people in one place, dancing, playing, or chatting; it can be quite a stimulus overload. If you are single, hopefully you have met someone at a munch who invited you out; if you haven't, then don't be shy, now is the time to be friendly and warm, and don't forget to smile. But how do you know what is acceptable behavior at a party? What happens if you are walking by and some adorable girl sheathed in latex has a bum that looks so good you just want to reach out and grab it?

Hang on there, tiger. Chances are she belongs to or is with someone and as a newbie you don't want to start off your new adventure by being blacklisted as someone who can't keep his hands to himself. A fetish party normally has very clearly posted rules about what is and is not acceptable behavior. Above all of them is this simple one; burn it into your brain and you will do fine:

Don't touch what isn't yours unless invited.

This goes for people's toys, slaves, Dominants; even their personal space might be an issue. If the fetish party is in a bar, then keep in mind what is acceptable in a public space like a bar—do you go groping any piece of ass that happens to walk by in a vanilla bar? Huh, huh? Not if you have half a brain. No, you are going to play nice with the other kids, be polite, and if you are new this is the time to network and get to know people. Chances are that if you want to be invited to private parties down the road then some of these people can make it happen. As I've mentioned earlier, in this community word travels fast. You want to be known as a positive person who has a lot to offer, not some letch that is selfish and doesn't understand boundaries. And for god's sake don't get drunk your first night out! You will normally find that people in BDSM have such heavy control issues that in the set-up play space most will be drinking bottled water. We want our public play to be safe and fun. If you don't know anyone at all, introduce yourself and ask questions. If you are polite and fun to be around you will be around for a long time. If you are the drunken little hussy, you will find someone to take you home but chances are that is not a rep you want to have. Play evenings are about fun; people are there for a good time and will welcome you if you demonstrate you are a positive person to be around. Chapter 5 will look at connecting with other like-minded kinky people in more detail.

D/s: Domination/submission.

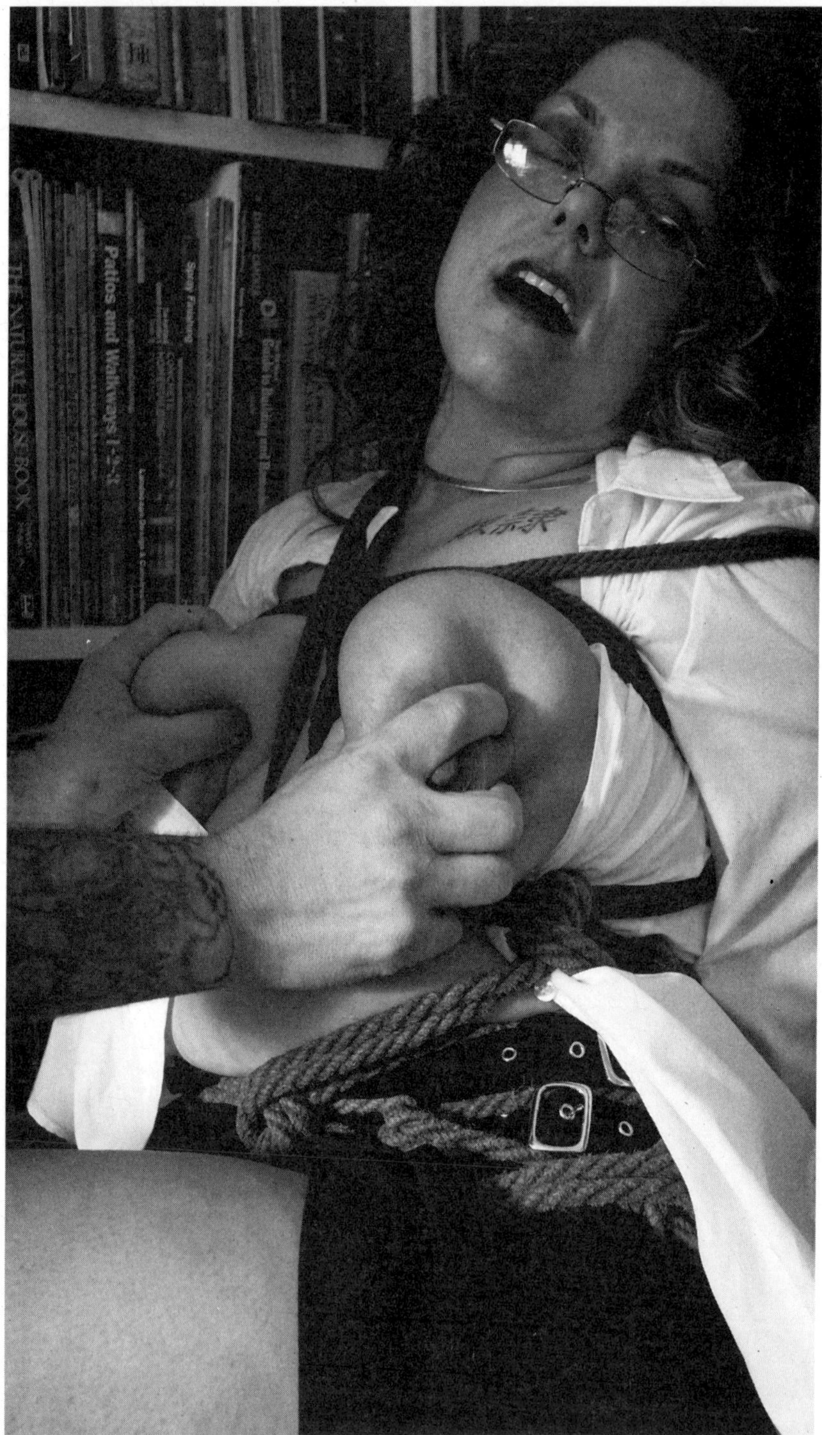
THE NATURAL HOUSE BOOK
Patios and Walkways

Chapter 4

What's on the Menu: All about Negotiation

What do you want? What does your play partner want?

How can you both get what you want and at the same time have fun? Communication is expressing what you need, and then listening to the other person. Listening with an open mind will help you build trust and figure out how best you can explore different areas together.

Wear Panties, Give a Foot Massage: Finding Middle Ground

When you have a potential partner who is interested in playing, and you get each other hot and bothered, how do you figure out what you are comfortable with and vice versa? How are you going to get your needs met while the other person's get met too? You might really be into someone, and he is into you, but your interests don't synch up entirely. It happens and is normal. What do you do? First of all it depends on the level of commitment or interest. For married couples or people in a long-term committed

Dungeon: A room or full studio that is equipped with BDSM toys and equipment.

relationship looking to spice up their sex lives, there will probably be things one partner is interested in that the other isn't. I suggest that if your partner is really into something specific, and it doesn't cross any personal boundaries with you, go ahead and indulge her. Then ask her to indulge you. For example, your husband comes to you and says, "Oh god, I really want to be cross-dressed and made to worship your feet, honey." If that scenario doesn't hold much interest for you, but it really doesn't turn you off, give it a try. The worst that is going to happen is hubby wears your panty hose and you get a foot massage. How tough is that to deal with? And if he gives you a decent foot massage, you send him off to learn how to give you a proper pedicure! This is a skill that can spill over into your everyday life—wouldn't it be nice to have someone pamper your feet after a hard day at work, and all for the cost of some panty hose, panties, and maybe an hour of your time? If you can keep an open mind about your partner's fantasies, you can usually intertwine them with yours. Of course you should also be willing to let the shoe (pardon the pun) be worn on the other

Digital cameras are a great way to explore your fantasies without having awkward conversations with a photo lab cashier.

foot. If you have a deeply held desire to be strapped into tight bondage and ravished sexually, then communicate your desires so you both can work toward a situation where you can find middle ground that will serve both your interests. If you want someone to be open minded and willing to listen to your desires, you have to be willing to listen to hers. Negotiating *can* be a win-win situation. This chapter will help you figure out what is important to you, and how to discuss it with a potential partner in such a way that there are no hurt feelings.

Edge Play: Play between partners that you might see at an event that will be beyond your own comfort level and can have an element of danger involved: fire, knives, et cetera. Experienced Edge Players typically will have sought out the DM/PM before playing to go over the house rules.

Trust Me

The word that frames this chapter best is *trust*. When you are asking someone what his interests are or sharing your most deeply held desire with him, you need to extend the comfort of trust to that person. If someone is going to let you tie her up and do all sorts of mean, nasty and wonderful things to her, I guarantee you that trust is the biggest issue of all. There has been a lot of writing about the "gift of submission" in contemporary BDSM literature, and it certainly has its merits, but I prefer the word *trust* because it indicates that trust needs to be extended from both parties and is not just a one-way dynamic such as a *gift*. A Dominant or Top also has to know that he can trust the submissive or bottom to let him know that he or she is in or outside of her boundaries and is willing to extend the courtesy to him of trusting that those boundaries will be accepted and honored. Trust is a fragile thing; it can be broken and disappear in a heartbeat when someone is careless—that is what gives it such value. Recognizing how special the moment is while you're pushing the other's limits in kinky sex is going to require that you build trust between you both.

The bedroom or dungeon should be a sanctuary where you can open your heart and emotions to your partner and express what you really desire without fear of retribution or shame. Everyone's sexuality is important. As individuals we need to own our sexuality and understand what makes us tick before expecting someone else to provide what we need. If you cannot communicate it effectively, how is your partner supposed to know what gets you off? You can't expect someone to read your mind and know intuitively what your hot buttons are. That leads to unrealistic expectations.

Rights and Responsibilities with Your Play Partner

You have the right to have your sexuality respected and not belittled, nor judged.

You have the right to have a safe space in which to explore your fantasies.

You have the right to physical, emotional and mental safety regarding your desires.

You have the right to say no.

You have the right to say yes.

Most of all, you are responsible for respecting all of these rights as they apply to your partner, if you want to create and build trust.

> After fifteen years of marriage we discovered BDSM, and we already had an exciting, satisfying sex life. Bringing kink into our lives was a fun, natural extension of our sexuality. However, the needs or standards of the relationship are tested on a regular basis. Those issues can change on a daily basis and it has been a few years and we are still figuring it all out as we move along, learning more and more about each other. It is definitely a process that is constantly evolving. We haven't figured it all out yet, but we love what we share and already have a committed relationship and that gives us the framework to be able to explore each other's fantasies.
>
> —cat and Rat, sub/Dom couple

Negotiating with a Play Partner

Are you going to negotiate as an "adult" or let your "bratty persona" do the negotiating for the scene? When you are new to exploring this, I suggest you work on building the skills of negotiating as an "adult" who is well balanced, someone who can take the time to listen carefully to what his partner needs and wants and also be able to express his own needs and desires. As you become more experienced with specific partners and the groundwork of negotiating limits has been established, you can start to explore your persona's character and limits. It really depends on the context of what is being explored. Negotiating real boundaries should be done as an adult, prior to the scene, but playful negotiation can

Enema: Gently introducing water into the bowels through a nozzle inserted into the anus. Used for either pleasure or humiliation depending on the context of the scene.

Relax and have fun with your kinky playtime. Laugh and enjoy.

Face Sitting: A practice where the Domme sits on the face of the submissive, forcing them to perform oral sex or "smothering" them. Can be used with or without clothing such as panties or leathers.

be part of the role-playing, *i.e.*, the sub might argue as a bratty schoolgirl bargaining to get out of a spanking from the headmistress at a private school.

> With any curious submissive or vanilla woman that I have met, honesty has always played the most important role in that dynamic. The first thing I do is tell her about my lifestyle and usually she becomes intrigued and then more curious. It can be an interesting position to be in, introducing a curious vanilla woman to my lifestyle. I try to get to know her likes and dislikes and find out if she has ever experienced anything like bondage or spanking. If we are dating and she wants to explore in a safe, controlled and sensual way, I create a small, safe scene to experiment with every item or area that raises her interest. I try to find out what she likes; this also gives me the opportunity to see if she likes what I like. I use positive, encouraging tones because I know newbies are a little hesitant and can tend to be in a more sensitive emotional state. Experimenting for the first time can make people nervous—they are letting their long-held desires finally bubble to the surface. I want to keep hurt feelings at bay and I always consider this to be an experimental phase. I don't have any expectations or make demands—it is just about exploring in fun and satisfying ways. —Joe, Master

Sometimes people's interests just don't match up and no amount of bargaining can result in a compromise. Someone's interests or limits might be beyond the scope of her partner's interests or personal limits. If this is the case, you should both avoid any blaming or judgmental language. This is also an opportunity for you to recognize your need to pursue these interests, if they are important enough, with others who are into them. This is a tricky area for those who are just getting into kinky play. An established couple might feel that their personal lives could be compromised if they play with others, and the best way to handle this situation is to establish personal boundaries that are not compromised through

The eyes are the window to the soul's desire.

Feminization: Enforcing behaviors or activities on a male submissive or slave that are normally associated with a woman. For example: cross-dressing him in female clothes, making him sit to urinate. Can be used for humiliation play or for empowerment depending on the context.

play. Some couples I know have very specific limits regarding play-time with others outside their personal dynamic. This is an ongoing negotiation in your personal lives. What are you comfortable with your partner doing? What is he or she comfortable with you doing? How can you discuss it without hurting each other's feelings? The key to this is using the "Oreo" method of discussion—sandwiching the challenging aspect of a situation between two positive points. Any "I" language should be positive feedback, *i.e.*, "I really love what we share; you are a fantastic woman and it is amazing when you spank me. But lately I have really been feeling that I would like to be taken advantage of by multiple hands while you are spanking me. How would you feel about finding a few people that would pinch, tickle and slap me while you are doing it? It would be really hot to know you are telling others what to do to me." Be sensitive to your partner when you bring this subject up and stress that it isn't "her fault" that she isn't able to provide what you desire from time to time. Nurturing the primary relationship

Fetish: Specific obsession or delight in an object *i.e.*, shoe fetish.

you are in, and not jeopardizing it for a secondary or tertiary relationship will help keep play dynamics fun and easier to manage without hurting others. There is a reason that you are in the primary relationship after all, but it is okay if you can't meet *all* the needs of your partner. Take time to figure out what each of you is comfortable with the other doing. I personally have a standing agreement within my primary relationship that we are both free to "safely do whatever you feel comfortable with having me do." Involving your other in the decision or boundary making process helps nurture the relationship.

> Leo and I don't so much negotiate as navigate: we sit down and talk our way through new situations as they come up, rather than trying to map things out before they happen. The bottom line is and always has been respect. We respect each other, whether in role or in our day-to-day life. I think that's a constant in all successful relationships, in business life, personal life, scene and vanilla. One of Leo's work colleagues, a very perceptive woman, recently told him that people have noticed he seems different when I'm around. Folks don't know why this alpha male is suddenly so attentive, more quiet, and subtly deferential to his wife. It makes them uncomfortable because they don't understand the change. Our dynamic is so natural to us that we really never noticed, and probably those who only know us as a couple would find it normal. Me, I just assumed this is the way men in love act toward their wives.
>
> —Violet (Violet and Leo met in the scene, became Mistress and submissive, and eventually fell in love and got married. They've been together for almost ten years.)

Negotiation is a skill that can help you in all aspects of your life. Inside or outside the bedroom, good communication will allow you to have your needs fulfilled as well as be empathetic to your partner's needs. If you work on communicating and negotiating you can both be fulfilled as a couple.

Sometimes the hottest kinky play is improvised on the spot with what you have on hand. A belt and some rope can be more than enough to get your playtime started.

Fetish Party: A chance to dress up and play with a large group of people usually at a club and a hell of a lot of fun!

What amazes me about "vanilla" people and their relationships is that they sometimes have problems with boundaries that are quite contrary to the negotiations that happen with play partners. Specifically, I have a cousin who took his wife's friend to a house party because his wife wasn't feeling well. Afterward his wife was upset because "he should know better than to take my friend without asking," but if they never discussed boundaries,

Fisting: Inserting the entire hand into the vagina or anus. When done properly it is easier to accomplish than most people realize. The term "fisting" is misleading as the hand is inserted slowly, with lots of lubricant, with the fingers formed into a gentle point. Only after the hand is in is it formed into a gentle fist.

how was he to know? As an experienced submissive, I find that open communication is essential to keeping things on track. Boundaries are discussed in a frank and open way and always in a respectful tone. That is one of the things I really like about the scene—people tend to work hard on communicating with others in polite, respectful ways without judgment or assumptions.

—gregg, submissive extraordinaire

Let's skip ahead to a time when you might be at a fetish night or a play party. How do you figure out if that hot little thing you just met is into some of the same things you are? Easy: ask her. Do it in a nonthreatening and casual manner and listen to what he or she is saying and then you can determine if those interests dovetail with your own. What you shouldn't do is compromise your own boundaries or comfort level just because you want to play and are intensely attracted to this person. No one should try to make you do things that are beyond your boundaries, including yourself. Respect where you are in your own skill level and know what your boundaries are. Remember too that negotiation can be more than just verbal; there are signs and body language that come into play when negotiating with someone new that you both should concentrate on in order to decipher just what is really being said.

My personal approach to negotiating a scene is both verbal and physical. The verbal components address the following about my prospective playmate: (a) are there any physical illnesses, *i.e.*, Hep C, STDs; or restrictions, i.e., torn rotator cuff, high blood pressure, diabetes; (b) are there any psychological issues, *i.e.*, Post Traumatic Stress Disorder, disassociation; (c) what safewords are to be used and what do the safewords mean? (d) is pain to be a component of the play and if so is pain to be managed through the use of safewords? (e) what styles of play are not acceptable (heavy percussion, cutting/branding/needles, breath play, restrictive play such as bondage/gagging, et cetera)? and finally (f) what form of aftercare will

Dirty girls need a good cleaning once in a while.

Flogger: Multitailed whip with flat ends used for erotic playtime. Usually made from leather, rubber, fur or rope.

be provided? The remaining critical verbal question I will ask as the Dominant, is: "What's in it for me?" I require my prospective playmates to tell me in a succinct way what it is they will give me in return for my investment in playing them. If I do not hear a response that touches my psyche then the negotiations end then and there. The physical communication is both prior to, during, and after play. If I do not observe signs of submission in these individuals' tone of voice and posture, a sincere, reverent look in their eyes, then I am prone to lose interest in playing with them. During play I continue to look for the body language conveyed by submissives. Do they

1 Choose a pair of your kinkiest boots or high heels. The hotter the better.

2 Standing in front of your submissive, order him to his hands and knees at the feet of his goddess.

move their body in a manner that reaches toward my toys or touches? Do they simply lie like a lump on the bench? Do they breathe in a manner that conveys an awareness of my presence, my caress, my slap? Do they communicate through facial expressions such as smiles, grimaces?

—Kindred, sadist/therapist

Being up front and honest about your needs will gain you respect. Be prepared to find that sometimes your own interests will not match up with those of someone else to whom you are attracted. It happens, and it doesn't necessarily mean you need to change.

Sometimes things can go wrong—we are, after all, only human. Boundaries can be crossed by accident or stumbled over, and how you deal with this is what is going to demonstrate your character or lack of it. When people are feeling emotionally tender you need to be tender back. You have to show them that when they are feeling vulnerable and fragile you will hold them and

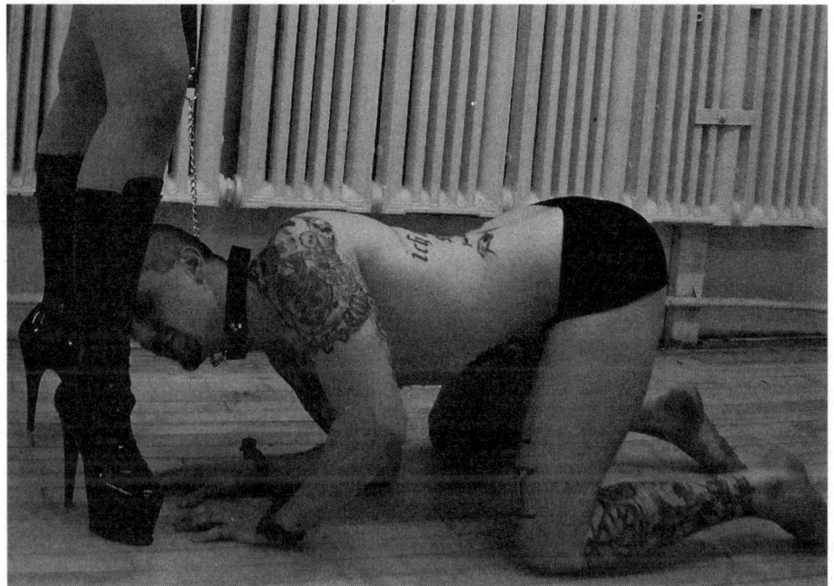

3 Tell him he is on trial and has to do a proper job or else he'll be punished and won't be given another opportunity to worship you. Continues→

reassure them. What you should not do is challenge them if a boundary has been crossed. Relax; take a breath and just chill for the time being until you can both discuss it as mature adults. Please don't fight fire with fire when a boundary has been crossed. Mean what you say and stick to it; show them you will follow through on what you say you will.

I can say that only one scene has ever gone really wrong for me. A new bottom was so eager to play with me that he misrepresented his interests, abilities and hard limits. After negotiating with him a number of times I invited him over for an afternoon of fun. I had told him what I enjoyed and what I expected to make a scene work for me. He often repeated how much he wanted to serve me and how he'd do anything for me. While some of his interests did nothing for me I believed that we had enough common ground to have an enjoyable afternoon. Right from the start, the scene wasn't progressing well

4 Encourage him to start with kissing the toe, with warm and nonslobbery pecks on the tip.

5 Have him slowly work his way up your calf, paying special attention to the firm muscles.

and at one point I asked him if there was something I could do to turn things around. He made a suggestion and I played along, hoping to salvage this scene. He then took over and started asking all these questions; if I didn't answer them as he liked he'd ask another, cutting me off. I ended the scene with a firm, "I'm not comfortable with this." He got dressed and asked me if I wanted to see him again. I was still in a bad head-space because I'd never had a scene go so unsatisfactorily. Throughout the scene the feedback I got from him was negative; I had gotten nothing of what was important to me; and he ended up the scene with trying to top from the bottom which was *not* part of what we had previously agreed upon. I took the polite approach and told him I wanted to think about it and he immediately bolted for the door. A couple of hours later he sent a very nasty text message to my cell phone. Had I been a newbie to play, this would have surely scared me away from the lifestyle for years if not permanently. I've since done

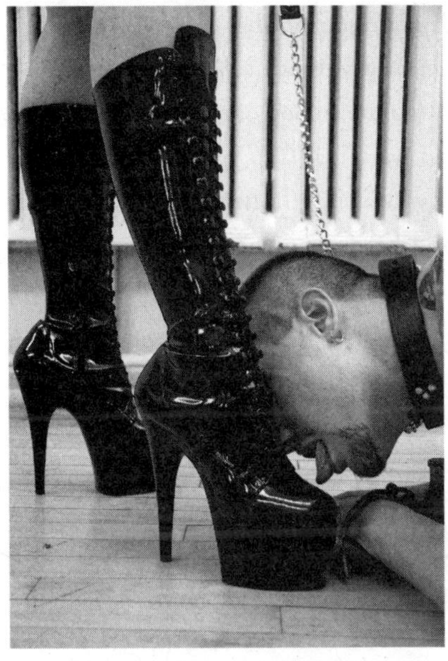

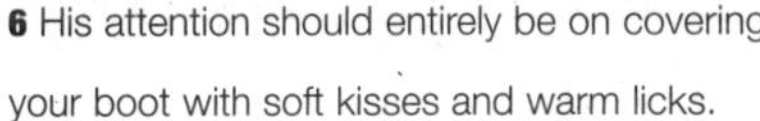

6 His attention should entirely be on covering your boot with soft kisses and warm licks.

7 Keep him focused with positive reinforcement: "Good boy, worship your goddess's boots."

> more reading and attended workshops on scene negotiating and other skills. I now expect much more concrete information from my bottoms before I play with them and I make sure that our interests are more compatible.
>
> —Mercury Kittie, Domme

When negotiations fall apart it is because of a lack of communication and understanding. Dialoging with your partner is essential. If you are asking for feedback before or during a scene, and you feel you are being pushed in a direction that you don't want to go or previously hadn't negotiated, then a little "time-out" never hurt anyone. Slow is easy. There is no rush; play should be *fun*—that is why it is called *play.* You also have the right to not accept play that isn't working for you. Perhaps you have a long-term partner with whom you are playing, and there is something that isn't quite working for you during a scene and you want to renegotiate. How do you salvage it and save yourselves any embarrassment? Easy:

you tell him. Again, the bedroom/dungeon should be a place where anything can be said or discussed without any fear of reprisal—where you can say, "Wait a minute honey, that ball gag really is making my jaw sore in a bad way," or "Can you grab that pillow and put it under my ass so you can get a better angle?" If your delivery is compassionate and kind, then it can be expected that your partner will hand you the pillow or adjust the ball gag and then you can continue. If you come across as a demanding asshole then that will pretty much kill the playtime right there. Adults negotiate, children whine.

Things to Remember

- ✔ Know your own interests and where your personal boundaries lie.
- ✔ Be empathetic and sensitive to your partner's interests without a judgmental attitude.
- ✔ Communicate your needs initially verbally and later with your body language.
- ✔ Communication lines should always remain open.
- ✔ Sometimes interests don't match.

As a Dominant or Top during the scene it is your job to keep the momentum of playtime going, and as a bottom you have a responsibility to communicate with the Top. It is also perfectly okay to request a time-out. I was doing an intense scene with a partner once when I inadvertently stumbled across an emotional trigger for her—one that she hadn't even known about. She started crying and not in a good way. I unbuckled her from the St. Andrew's cross, scooped her up in my arms, and lay down with her on the bed and just held her while she cried. It happens, and this point will be discussed in more detail in chapter 8, Safety. Eventually she calmed down and we talked about what had happened and decided that getting out of the dungeon, getting a bite to eat and talking about it would be the best thing right then. A few hours later, after I'd listened to her figure out what triggered her reaction, she suggested that we go back to the dungeon and try some lighter activity that was as far away from that trigger as possible. Just some nice spanking, as she was still really eager to play and having had a few hours of chilling-out time helped her to reflect on what was happening and why.

At the same time, it is not your responsibility to play therapist—in fact I would strongly caution you against it. Listening to someone talk out her issue or complication is what makes you a responsible and caring human being. Trying to force her to work out her problems along a timeline that is convenient for you so you can play again is not an activity I condone. If someone has a problem like the above example, let him or her take the lead in figuring things out. Be there for her and let her know that you are a safe person to share with. When things go awry it is important that you become the compassionate person you are for the person that is in distress, instead of "Mistress Ilsa, Conqueror of Lower Germania and All the People of It." You can go back to being the big bad Dominant later on. All of kinky play is only as real as you both make it.

Forced Orgasm: Orgasm(s) brought about against a person's control or will as part of "resistance play" that involves informed consent.

There also needs to be time set aside sometime afterward to discuss what happened during the playtime. Aftercare is covered in chapter 8, but just note that you should always schedule time to talk about what you liked, what worked, and what you would change for your next playdate. It shouldn't be at the event or right after the scene, but rather following some time for reflection, perhaps the next day, provided no boundaries were crossed and each of you were happy with what happened in the scene, whether at a public play party or in private. This discussion can range from expressions of satisfaction like "Oh, I loved it all, you are the bestest in the world!" to the two of you lingering for an hour, talking about the yummy and not so yummy things that happened. In my life I make it very clear to my playdates that I expect to hear from them the next day. If I don't, then I will be following up.

Sometimes people may not have any negative reaction until the next day, after they have had a chance to process what took place, and I don't want anyone to be in a bad headspace, afraid to call me and discuss what is going on. Be responsible as a Dominant or Top—show them that they are just as important after the scene as they were during it. Conversely, I also like to hear about the yummy things that they enjoyed: that way I can start to plan and build the next scene in my mind. Getting to know what someone likes and doesn't like gives you ideas for the next playdate!

Chapter 5

From Online to Real Life

Get offline.

No, really—get offline.

Shut the computer down and find other people that are into kinky sex. Find workshops run by sex stores, outreach programs or organizers of fetish events. There is a big, wide world out there of fetish- and kink-oriented events and experiences that online will never be able to compare to, ones that are full of human interaction and emotion. You can spend hours, weeks or years online and develop a false sense of expertise and security, or you can have real-life good times that will eclipse the cyber world. You've done yourself a favor by picking up this book, which at the very least is a tangible book to read that doesn't require servers and ISPs and a laptop with RAM blah blah blah and all that other technical stuff. You can read it on the bus or the subway. Or possibly at work on your lunch break where people will most certainly take note of the sexy cover and you might get one or two knowing glances.

Gates of Hell: A device for males that has a series of metal rings attached to a strap that is slid around the penis and then fastened at the base to deprive the male of sexual stimulation.

So how do you get offline?

Easy—go online and search.

I am not making this easy, am I?

Online is a great way to find resources, and discuss ideas and commonalities—but we live in the real world, and you can only go so far online. The Internet DOES offer a great deal from the point of view of resources. When I first started exploring the kink world, e-mail was still in its infancy. Now you can Google "BDSM events" and have thousands of links across the world pop up.

> It can be extremely hard to meet someone in real life that meets your kinky needs. The Internet provided me with a valuable resource for meeting like-minded friends and partners, giving me the chance to search by age, location, role and fetishes. It is important however, not to get stuck in an online fantasy world. I like to see it as a tool, but not a place for forming a relationship. No matter how compatible you may seem online, it doesn't mean you'll get along in person. I was lucky enough to find my Master on a bondage website, which then led to a face-to-face meeting. During our first few years together, as I struggled with my new role as a slave, it was forums on the Internet, and a few like-minded friends that helped me accept and learn all about this new part of me. I didn't feel that I could turn to my vanilla friends for advice because they didn't understand what I was going through or what it meant to be in a Master/slave relationship. Being able to read other slaves' experiences on online forums and blogs was helpful to me. You need other people that you can talk to freely without worry of judgment, who understand what you are going through. Having a group of friends that share a similar lifestyle is also important. —doll, slave

Feel Like a Munch?

A munch is a fantastic way to get started. What is a *munch?* It is a casual gathering, usually at a pub or restaurant, where other kinky folks come to meet and be social. One thing it is not is a place to play or show off toys or display how well you have trained your slave to kneel on the floor beside you eating out of the palm of your hand. These are evenings where people come to meet in a vanilla setting to discuss ideas, and share thoughts and experiences—but there is no play. So what is the point of just getting together and talking? I mean, come on, maybe you are all hot and bothered; possibly you have just bought your first set of wrist restraints and are dying to try them out. How about picking up someone that night, going somewhere together, and playing? Chill for a moment; I know you want to run headfirst into this world, but not so fast. A munch is not a pickup joint or a meat market. Its strength lies in the fact that there are many others with varied experiences that are willing to get together to talk about what works for them, what hasn't, what they want to try, and also what movie they went to see last Friday night. It is a great place to trade resources. I like to think of it as parallel to the experience of nomadic adventurers hundreds of years ago, meeting at an oasis, trading their information and knowledge. Exchanging ideas in an oral tradition is one of the strengths of the human race. It is one thing that has allowed us to thrive and grow and spread across the globe. You will find people like yourself that are new, others who have been playing for years, and still others that drop in from time to time. Please keep in mind that manners and politeness count.

Golden Shower: A form of play that involves urinating on your partner (or being urinated on).

> I was comfortable enough in the chatroom I was frequenting as a sub, but the whole time I was aware that it was all fantasy. I was itching to get out into the "real world." The idea of meeting people in real life that were similar to the online friends I had developed terrified me. I used my online search skills to find a local group in my town and decided to attend a munch and even requested that one of my online friends, a fantastic real-life Dom who was always coaxing me to come out to a munch, meet me there. After all, a munch is a public meeting, very informal, and any obvious signs that this was a BDSM

Grope Box: A box large enough to hold a person with many openings along its sides and top. A submissive or bottom is placed within it and then is groped or fondled by multiple people outside that they cannot see.

group were strictly prohibited. Swallowing the lump in my throat and sweating with nerves, when I got to the local pub I found my Dom friend already there chatting with everyone. He knew most of the BDSM community. I didn't have to ask which one he was, it was quite apparent by his natural ease in the crowd with others chatting to him. Making the rounds, I met with everyone and then sat down with him. He recognized how nervous I was, but knew that I was making the transition from online to real life. He also delicately quashed my notion that I had any level of experience whatsoever since it was just online experience. The munch was a VERY good idea. It was a safe place, familiar, and no play was taking place. I attended several munches, turning down offers to attend play parties at each meet; continued with my online chatroom group and strengthened my bond with my Dom friend. He took me to my first play party when I felt I was ready and I haven't looked back since.

—Jenny, Switch

Do everyone a favor when you head for the munch—leave the camera and notebooks at home. When people come to munches, there is the understanding that they will not be recorded. Some have vanilla careers or lives and would rather not have their kinky sides posted on Facebook or YouTube. You might be really excited to finally have a chance to meet people living in the lifestyle you have always dreamed about and want to share it on your blog, but people don't want to be outed and it is not your right to do so. Let me repeat that again—do NOT out anyone. Ever. Which means if you see someone at a munch and enjoy pleasant conversations with him or her or maybe not-so-pleasant conversations, then see that individual in the vanilla world with his spouse or coworker, he is trusting that you will NOT out him even if you had a really enthusiastic conversation regarding latex bodysuits. The other attendees at a munch are trusting that you will extend them the same privacy they would you. Tact and candor are virtues that will take you far in the kink world. You may exchange knowing glances in a public place but don't be offended if the person doesn't acknowledge you. She saw you; it's nothing personal, just let it go and wait until the next munch when you will see her again. Sometimes outsiders think of the BDSM/kink world like they do the Freemasons—as a secret society with its own conventions, rules, and regulations that should come with a secret handshake or signal. Sorry to say there isn't one, although that would be pretty cool.

Hard Limit: What someone absolutely will not do. Not negotiable.

When you pick a dildo for a strap-on, get one that looks and feels nice.

Hitachi Magic Wand: The greatest vibrator ever. Buy two.

No one has the right to out someone else—ever. If you are outed by someone you need to tell the organizer of the munch you attended and that person will be dealt with. All munches are run by an organization or an individual and the scene is very good at policing itself. You are also responsible for NOT nonconsensually involving others. You might have a really hot fantasy of leading your new slave down the street on a leash, but doing that will involve passersby, which is not only unfair to them but demonstrates you don't have any tact or common sense. You don't ask to experience others' fetish or interests when you aren't prepared for it, so don't do it in public to the "vanillas." Wait until the Pride Parade when the context is festive and anything goes and you can get away with frivolity like that. Again, good manners go a long way in the fetish world, just like in real life. You may feel like a god and demand to be revered as one at a party, but see how far that gets you. The community does have its sense of humor but it will also ostracize you for not complying with the codes of behavior that are acceptable or for being a dangerous person to be around. People in the community will always like to talk about drama, so don't air your dirty laundry. More than likely you will meet people that you are interested in playing with at a munch, but like I said—this is not a pickup joint. Spend time getting to know the people there, but don't run off with them immediately. In fact I caution strongly against that on the first meeting.

Ask others about someone who interests you in a casual way: "I noticed Princess Icewingdeath over there who said she is into rope bondage, is she a good Top?" Yes, sometimes we do call ourselves silly names! Some people have incredibly interesting and creative names. Like I mentioned before—this is all only as real as we want to make it. Do you want to be tied up and strapped down while Sir Vesuvius takes you to pleasures unknown, moment by delicious moment, your nerves on fire and your head spinning with endorphins as you burn each second of that evening into your memory...or do you want "Chuck from accounts receivable" to do it? Some people adopt a persona or a character, reveling in mystery while cloaking themselves to avoid vanilla issues that they would rather not have to deal with. Honor their right to have a persona and don't judge or question it.

> What "the community" means to me is a place of personal freedom, where you can express yourself without fear of judgment for your sexual desires. The community tends to be warm, welcoming, and can seem very "normal" on the surface. We are brought together by the community because of our differences. A munch can even seem quite boring and "normal"—in Canada, for instance, people spend more time talking about the weather than wild sex-fueled adventures. And when the subject does turn to wild adventures, they will discuss it with the same seriousness as the weather. I like to assist at various events because I believe it is important to give back to a community that has welcomed and encouraged me in my own personal growth as a Dominant.
>
> —Geordie, Dominant

Hobble Skirt: A long, tight skirt that ends below the knee, which restricts motion of the legs when walking. Results in the wearer walking slowly in a hobbling motion. Think Morticia Adams's skirt from "The Adams Family" TV show.

Models of Dominance and Submission

> While D/s deals with representations of brutality and cruelty, and the emotional responses to them, adherents are quick to point out that D/s is not about actual acts of brutality and cruelty. It is a consensual power exchange between the two partners and need not involve any brutality (such as corporal punishment) or cruelty (verbal or emotional abuse) at all. It is primarily based upon trust and communication between the partners. It is also based on a deep ethos of mutual respect in which exploration of the emotions brought up by brutality and cruelty can take place in a safe, sane and consensual manner. —wikipedia

All of BDSM is only as real as you want it to be or make it between you and your partner or potential partner(s). There are many different degrees of Dominant/submissive relationships:

Hood: A device to cover the head, either partially or completely, typically made of leather or PVC.

some are monogamous, and some are polyamorous or involving multiple partners. These terms can be applied to both the sexual dynamic as well as the emotional and mental ones. There are many models of dominance and submission. Which is right for you? First of all, your sexuality shouldn't define you, but it's definitely an important part of you, so ask yourself this easy question: "What do I want?" What are your personal interests or needs? Do you want to be the Daddy Dom? Do you want to be Catherine the Great? Do you have a desire to be a nurturing, sensual Dominant, or a hardcore prick who extracts his pleasure from a suffering body? Do you long to be tied up and used as a sex toy, an object of lust and passion from whose writhing flesh others take their pleasure? Are you a damsel in distress? Are you a hero? What if sexual play doesn't interest you but you love the fantasy of being a butler in charge of a household for the Master, or a lady-in-waiting? What about observing military protocol—with boots that are spit-polished and everything in its place?

Take a deep breath and remember this is a journey, not a destination. Your interests will be revealed as you take the time to explore. Before you jump into labeling yourself, figure out what attracts you and nudge your way into it. Meet and watch people at fetish events who are doing things that interest you, buy them a drink and see if they are willing to talk with you about what it is that interests them and how they approach it. I find that people love to talk about their favorite subject—themselves. Smile warmly and be sincere and more often than not if they have time they will be happy to share.

> At an event I might meet someone and identify myself as a "submissive" and their response might be "Oh great, I need my dishes done, be at my place at three p.m. tomorrow," and then the next step is we have to have a discussion on what "submissive" means to me. For example, "By 'submissive' I mean I enjoy giving my partner pleasure," et cetera.
>
> —gregg, submissive extraordinaire

Being put on display for the enjoyment of others is a common exhibitionist fantasy.

Safe Calls

One interesting transition from the kink crowd into the vanilla dating world is the concept of a *safe call.* A safe call is useful when you are getting ready to meet someone new—perhaps from the Web or after just having met them in a larger group. You call a friend and say, "Hey, I am meeting someone new at one p.m. for coffee. I will call you at three p.m. if everything is okay." That way if you don't call by three they know that they need to take the next step that you have instructed them to—such as calling you and listening for prearranged code words indicating either things are great, such as "Thanks for calling, Mom, I will see you next week," or, if you are in a very uncomfortable situation, "Mom, I need you to feed my cat." Your friend should know where you are going and what to do if you are in trouble. A first meeting in the real world should only be an hour or two for the initial contact. DON'T go home with this new acquaintance or off to play.

Safe calls have been around in the kink world for decades and

I am not surprised to see that the practice has spilled out into the vanilla dating world lately. Kinky people are very astute when it comes to meeting new people from the Web, especially when it comes to playtime that can involve sex out of the ordinary—things that are going to be used percussively, bondage, et cetera. A safe call takes a moment to set up and could get you out of a very uncomfortable or potentially dangerous situation. The person meeting you should also be aware that you have a safe call in place and a backup plan. An honorable person will agree to it and a dishonorable one will be offended.

First Date

Beyond arranging that safe call, you'll want the person you are going to meet to have the same qualities that would interest you in the vanilla world—trustworthiness, empathy, a fun person to be with; the kinky interest just kind of completes the package. Should you jump on a plane and rush across the country filled with passion from your online encounters, your belly fluttering

Sometimes your partner will WANT to be used like a hot piece of man-meat to satisfy your desires.

with anticipation of all you have longed for about to come true? Take a breath and take your excitement down a notch. We all have fantasies but we live in reality. One of the problems with developing an online "relationship" with someone is that he or she can present himself any way he likes and at your real-life meeting, he may not live up to your expectations. This is one of the reasons I caution against ongoing cyber affairs, regardless of distance. It is easy to be caught up in the excitement of your first date with a kinky person who matches "everything" your online list states. Ugh: those online lists—nice complete checklists that measure the wide range of human sexuality with little boxes. How much weight can you allow that? Some, granted that at least it gives you an idea what the person is into, but this is why I encourage people to go to munches and get involved in real-life experiences. It is too easy to become lost on the Internet.

When deciding where to meet them, you should agree on a public setting—a coffee shop in the mall or a restaurant where there are others around to assist if something isn't right. This is good common sense. Someone who is willing to meet you in a public place probably has her own safe call in place as well. Someone who wants you to come to his house for a first meeting, or get into her car when you first meet her, should be shown your ass...as you are walking away. Don't put yourself in an uncomfortable situation for a first meeting. Ever.

House Slave: A bottom or submissive who may or may not live with the Dom/me, who acts in a domestic role such as maid or butler service, performing household duties, often while naked. A sexual D/s relationship may or may not be a part of the arrangement.

Parties!

There are as many types of fetish parties as there are people. If you live in a metropolitan area, you usually have a variety of choices. Do you want the fetishy crowd where people show off their outfits and dance? Or do you want an event that concentrates on high protocol? Perhaps you want to see people play, and play hard? How do you present yourself as the new Dominant or new submissive without stepping on other toes? You don't have to pretend to know everything. If it is your first night out or you are new on the scene, find the host and introduce yourself as

Humiliation Play: Causing sexual arousal in your partner through elements of shame, humiliation or embarrassment. To be engaged in only consensually.

a newbie—"Hi, I am slave peter and this is my Mistress Queen Sheba. This is our first night out and we wanted to know how to act here so we don't act inappropriately. We would appreciate your advice." Being polite and having a smile will get you further than being demanding. Normally, if the host has time (and this is part of the duties of a host) he or she will be happy to introduce you to others and help you get your feet wet. Conversely, there is also something to be said for the voyeuristic approach—there is nothing wrong with being low key and just watching. If you are at an event with play equipment, there will usually be a set of rules posted regarding behavior.

So what are you going to see at your first fetish event? What exquisite fun things await you? You will hear the music pumping from the moment you walk up the stairs to the club—I always love that moment. There are a whole bunch of clubs that are near and dear to my heart but one particularly has a dingy, skanky feel to the stairway that thousands of bands, kinky people, and bar backs have trod time and time again. The moment I hit those dog-leg stairs I start thinking about what is going to happen that night, what might happen and what I hope will happen. My fingers trace the cracked plaster on the walls that have been rubbed raw with desire and expectations over the past one hundred years. After I've checked in with the security guards and handled the paperwork of signing the door list, the double doors open up and I see a sea of leather-sheathed bodies grinding to the music. Everyone is dressed to impress on the lower level. The stage show tonight has a grinder girl showering the crowd with sparks of fire—the show will rotate throughout the night with erotic burlesque, rope bondage suspension and the capper, a latex fashion show. There are pieces of equipment around the perimeter of the room that submissives are tied to or are climbing in an attempt to avoid their Mistresses' whips that sharply catch their tender flesh, only to raise their asses once again after the sting has faded. The tightly packed stairway leads to a dedicated play area with more crosses, benches and couches strewn about the room, being used by people in various modes of undress and play.

I love the socializing that I get to do at the club—I catch up with my friends old and new every two weeks like this, sharing skills or secret new rope ties I have figured out, and finding out what new things they have been up to. The community is out in full force on these evenings and there is eye candy everywhere as the girls primp and preen, as well as some of the men. All-black-wearing Masters are countered gracefully by Mistresses in tight-laced corsets and long flowing gowns. Submissives and slaves are sometimes naked, or sometimes dressed the way their owners' desire. A tantalizing sea of flesh pulses both to the music heard and to their own beat almost until the sun comes up.

Insertables: Anything inserted into a bodily opening—*i.e.* the ass, pussy or mouth—for sexual purposes. Butt plugs, dildos—all Insertables should be covered with a condom before play.

As someone who has always engaged with her sexuality in an almost purely academic fashion and who has made a serious commitment to educating people about safer sex practices, my first appearance at and adventure into Toronto's fetish and BDSM scene was an eye-opening one! My penchant for all things dramatic, my synchronous passions for both performance and voyeurism, coupled with my innate curiosity about all things sexual and my love of a good story resulted in my securing press passes to SWITCH, Northbound Leather's annual fetish party, held in Toronto in 2007. I was fortunate to have been exposed to some of the more classic elements of fetishism and BDSM via a seminar taught by Professor Leslie Katz at the University of Toronto. Consequently, nothing I encountered at SWITCH was truly shocking, ranging from the full-body PVC costumes, to the St. Andrew's crosses, to the rather excellent bootblacking service. What I was unprepared for and found pleasantly surprising was the politeness, tact and appreciation for personal space that the general population at the event embodied and maintained. In other club spaces, and as a relatively diminutive woman of color, negotiating one's personal space can be a challenge at best and a traumatic experience at worst. At SWITCH, in an environment where I was virtually sur-

Infantilism: Role-play in which the adult participant takes on the role of an infant, dressing in diapers and engaging in infant play with toys or sucking on a pacifier. See Role-Play.

rounded by a primarily male and Caucasian crowd I felt the safest I'd ever been in a club setting. It is incredibly refreshing to know concretely on a deeply personal instead of removed academic level that within the fetish community, active open communication about what is and isn't personally acceptable, safe, sane and consensual isn't just encouraged, it's desirable and incredibly sexy.

—Niya B., Chair Elect, 2007–2008, Sexual Diversity Studies Students' Union, Mark S. Bonham Center for Sexual Diversity Studies, University of Toronto

As we learned in chapter 3, there is one universal rule at a fetish event, and that is *Don't touch what isn't yours unless invited.* This means toys or other people. Kinky people are sticklers for boundaries and will enforce them. If you grab someone's ass at a nightclub or try to fondle him or her, you usually get a slap or the bouncer will escort you to the door. If you try it at a fetish event, keep in mind most people are carrying striking implements with them to begin with.

You will usually find a play area separate from the socializing area, with dungeon equipment set up at various stations. There will be a PM (Play Monitor) or DM (Dungeon Monitor) person walking the perimeter, making sure the rules of public play are adhered to. They won't be intrusive to those playing and enjoying themselves in the scene. Normally they will have an identifying red armband, and their role is to provide immediate assistance if there is a safety issue, especially if first aid is required (and for those hosts that read this book, I would strongly advise you to select people as PMs or DMs that have training in first aid). They also ensure that the code words for the evening are known to everyone who enters to play. There are various regional differences but what is becoming the universal standard is: "Green, Yellow, and Red." The use and meaning of these code words will be covered more fully in chapter 8, Safety. Importantly, they direct the traffic in the play area, keep track of who is waiting in line for equipment and make sure there is no one bothering the

Latex outfits hug the body in all the right places and for those who fetishize it there is nothing hotter.

Inversion Table: A flat table the submissive can be bound to that pivots so that the submissive can be rotated upright or upside down.

après players in the cooldown area. If you want to know if there is a waiting list for a particular piece of equipment, just find one of the red-banded monitors and ask nicely. Seldom will there be people queued behind the St. Andrew's cross—that would ruin the vibe for those playing on it. The PM or DM will keep a mental note or have some way of keeping track of who is in the queue.

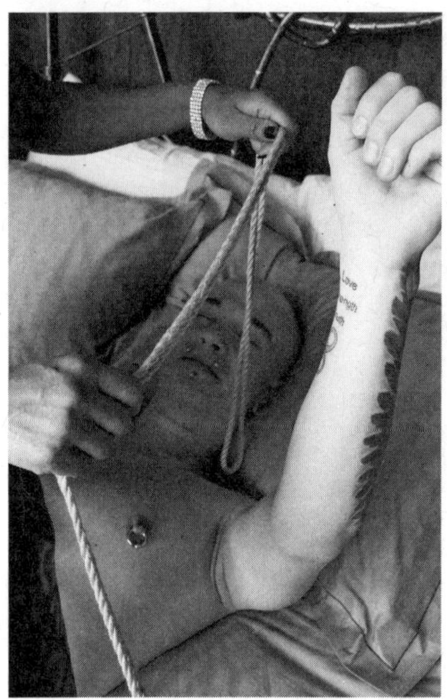

1 Find the middle of the rope and fold it over so it is doubled.

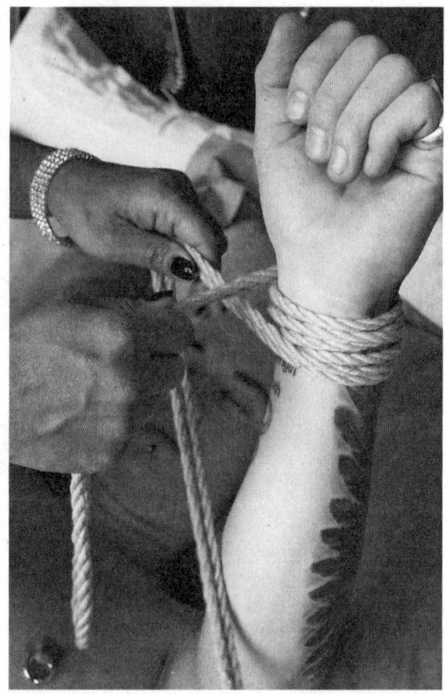

2 Wrap it around their wrist three times, leaving about a 12" tail where the looped (also known as the "bight") end is.

Who becomes a PM or DM? PMs and DMs are volunteers from the community that want to give back to the scene. It is an unpaid job but certainly not thankless. It is filled by experienced players who do a shift for about one to two hours. If you want to learn how to be a PM or DM, tell the host you would be interested in being a part of the next event and ask how you can do so. If you are a newbie you will shadow an experienced PM and DM until you satisfy the host's requirements before being allowed to have a shift on your own. It is also a really great way to meet people in the scene at events since you will be forced to interact with them.

Recently I volunteered at a BDSM market event held in Atlanta, a fundraising Bake Sale for the National Coalition for Sexual Freedom. Every room and corner was stuffed with sensual merchandise. People from all walks of life began to pour through

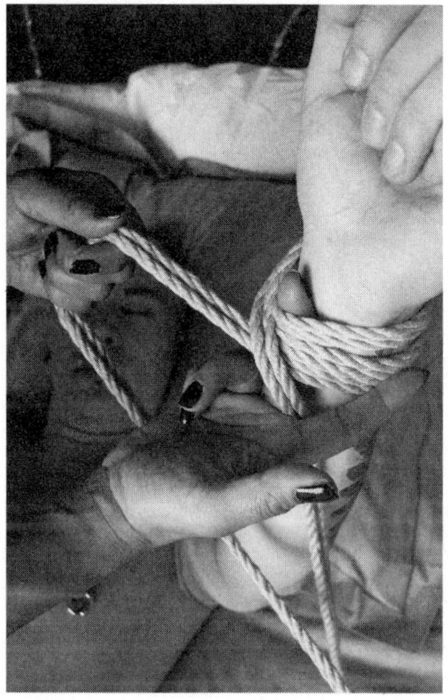

3 Your wraps should be loose enough that you can fit a finger up through them.

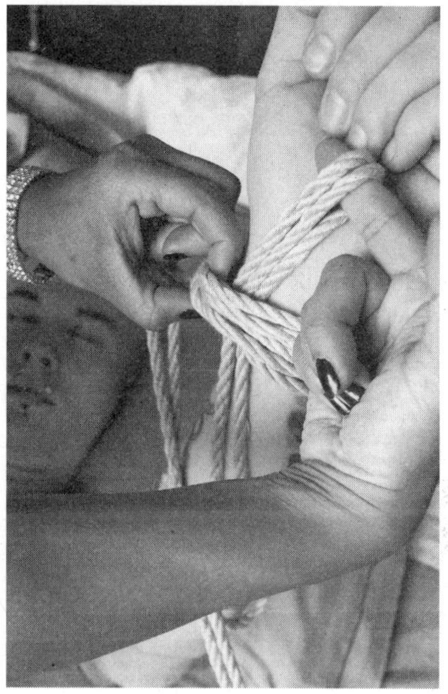

4 Cross the loop end of the rope over the other end then firmly pull it up through the wraps (up against the skin). Continues→

the double doors. There were lots of new faces as well as folks I had seen before at parties and munches.

People were wandering around in various states of titillation and disinterest. It hit me that I was standing in this booth designed to support the protection of "Sexual Freedom." *Okay,* I thought, *let's test it!* The next "customer" was a woman looking like anybody I'd meet at the grocery store. She was paying me no mind and trying to read over a cake label. I made a slight move toward her and got her attention. "Did you hear about our special? Between now and four o'clock, every person that purchases a goody to support the National Coalition of Sexual Freedom gets a free bonus. If you are so inclined, you are invited to grope or be groped by me." She cocked her head slightly then smiled. She turned her head back to the table of sweets and said, "I'll take a slice of pie and those cookies." When the

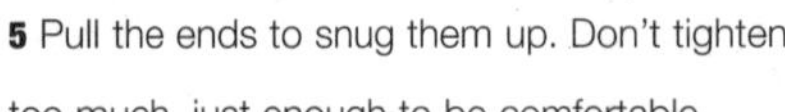
5 Pull the ends to snug them up. Don't tighten too much, just enough to be comfortable.

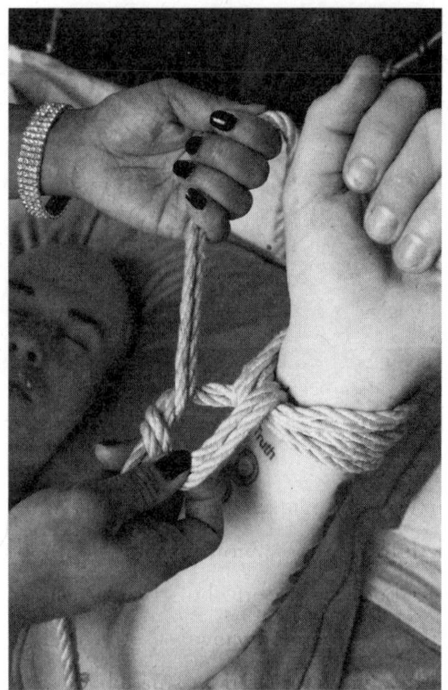

6 Tie the ends in a simple double knot.

bakery transaction was completed, she emptied her arms and put them down by her side, lifted her shoulders back to display her breasts, and stepped toward me and proclaimed, "All right, now YOU may please ME." The only difference between an ordinary situation and an extraordinary situation is just that little extra. For the next fifty minutes, I had the most awesome opportunity to get a spectacular and personal view into a diverse group of people's lives. How much time would it have taken me to get that much information if I had opted to limit my search to www.insertnameofkinkycruisingwebsitehere.com?

—Artemis Hunter, hetero-flexible Switch

There are a lot of different issues that arise when you first start getting into kinky sex, such as: how do you deal with vanilla issues in a scene and how do you deal with scene issues in vanilla life? There are people involved in this lifestyle in 24/7 roles of

7 Tighten the knot.

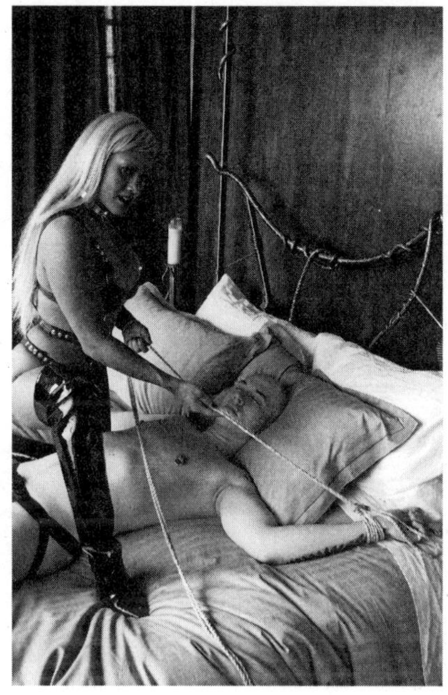

8 Lay their arm out toward the bedpost that you are going to tie them to. Continues→

Master/Mistress and slave and newbies usually wonder, how did they get to the point where they have that kind of relationship? Other issues such as, should you punish a recalcitrant submissive that is being bratty and doesn't want to do what you asked him to? What if you are at a party and she does something to embarrass you? These questions are easy to answer. First of all, compassion is essential in any human relationship. That has to be above all else and always foremost in your mind. Second, picking someone to be involved with who has a low drama threshold is a great way to avoid certain obvious speed bumps. Remember, these are roles we are playing with at fetish events. If someone is making demands outside the boundaries you have established or agreed upon, there is nothing wrong with you taking him aside (always do it away from an audience) and saying "Red—you are not within the boundaries that we agreed upon and you are making me uncomfortable. This is your only warning before I stop with you." If the other person

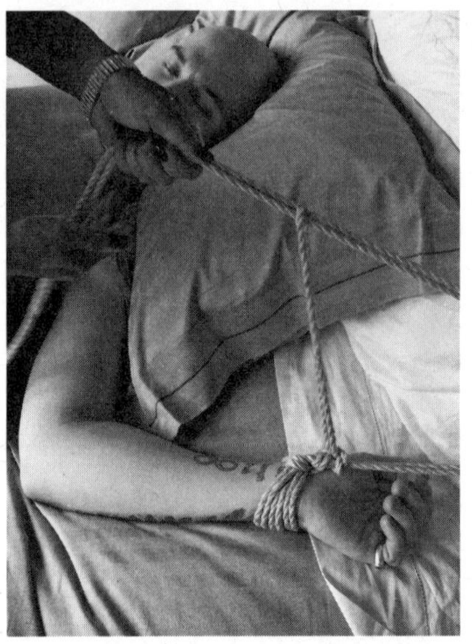

9 Loop the long end around the bedpost and then feed that end through the loop that you left, which should be about 8" long now that you have used it to make a double knot.

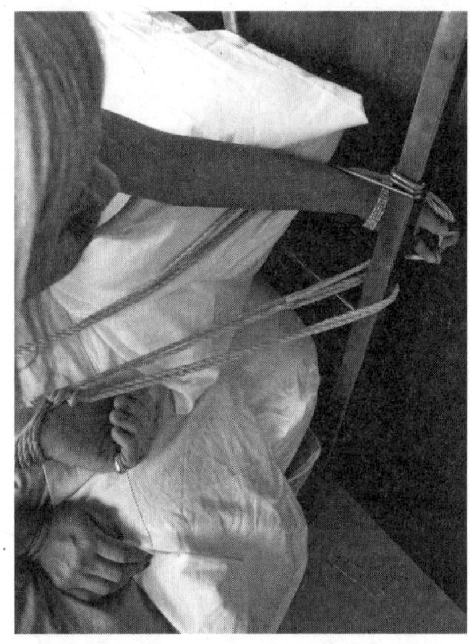

10 Once you have the long end through the loop, go back around the bedpost and come to the loop end.

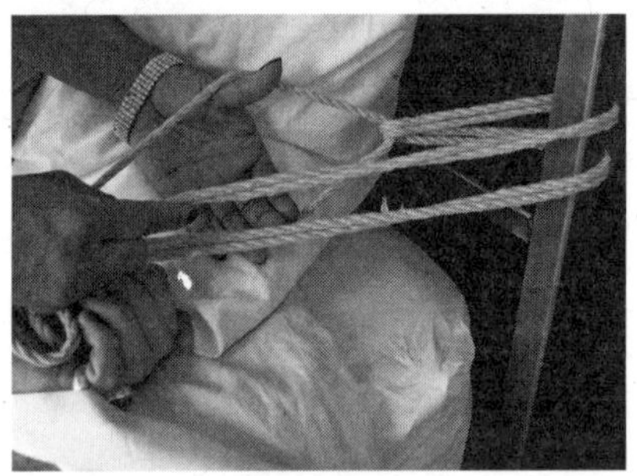

11 Perform a nice easy overhand hitch through the looped end and finish with a quick release knot.

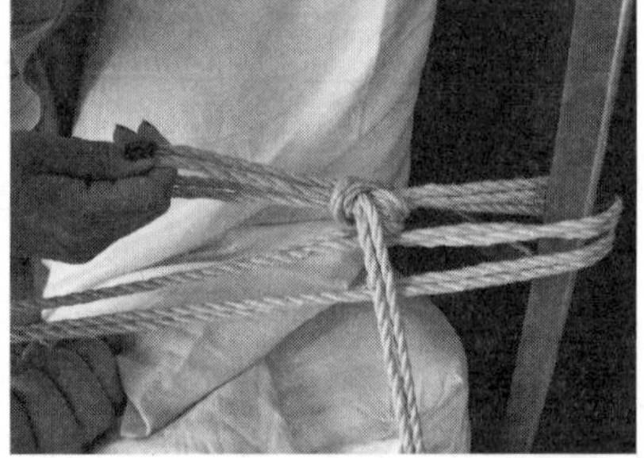

12 This is also known as the "Redneck Trucker's Knot" and will give you easy access to tighten or loosen it when fucking "on the fly."

continues his behavior then you can let the whole role drop—remember the old adage: the best way to punish a masochist is by not punishing them. You ALWAYS have the choice to leave a situation if it isn't right. Always. No one should ever cajole you into playing if you don't feel up to it. I have had more than several instances where

I was looking forward to a fetish party all week long and at the last minute my date and I weren't feeling the vibe to play when we walked in the door. That is okay—truly it is. Don't get bitchy and demanding, or try to coerce someone into play just because you are all hot and bothered. Sometimes the vibe isn't there and that is cool—there are lots of ways to enjoy yourself at a fetish event; you don't HAVE to play. Use your time to socialize more, network, or even simply dance.

Japanese Bondage: A style of rope bondage that originated from the Far East, particularly Japan, that is characterized by elaborate patterns of rope used to restrain and stimulate the submissive.

> Many times I have gone out to dinner or a party with a slave or two in lifestyle mode, even dressed in a manner that would raise interest from those involved in the lifestyle, but well within acceptable boundaries of the vanilla world. My dates, or slaves, are always instructed to act appropriately. There was one incident that required me to do a bit of damage control. How you deal with scene issues if they come up in vanilla life is based on your integrity. I had a slave who was new and eager to please, and in her eagerness, the first time she was meeting my family she addressed me as "Master" in front of them. I had to explain this crazy lifestyle to them afterward, about how it is all consensual between adults and that it was a real turn-on for both her and me. I promised she wouldn't do it again and make them feel uncomfortable. Then she and I had a long talk about what is important to me and my boundaries and that I understood she was new and eager but that being my slave didn't give her license for her brain to take a holiday; on the contrary, serving me would require her to be on the ball more than ever. Thankfully my family accepted our relationship and didn't even raise an eyebrow over it all, having suspected I was into kinky sex since college. Personally I believe extreme honesty in all phases of this lifestyle is essential for one's growth potential.
>
> —Joe, Master

Sometimes you might witness activities at a party that you are uncomfortable with. What is allowed at some venues isn't allowed

Kami: A technique that involves tying the hair. Often times rope will be braided into long hair and then used to keep the head in one place.

at others. When two experienced people are getting ready to do some "edge play" at a party, they will have already checked with the PM or DM before entering the play area. There are some really wild and imaginative things people get into—you can do wonders with a role of plastic wrap, olive oil, thirty inches of surgical tubing and a hairbrush. If you aren't comfortable with what you're seeing, then turn and walk to a different part of the room, or if you are really uncomfortable, then pick up your coat and leave. What you shouldn't do is cause a commotion. If you see what you perceive as the abuse of a slave in front of the room in the play area, you don't have a clue what the real dynamic is that's going on between the people involved in the scene. Perhaps the submissive enjoys degradation or cruelty. It is not for you to judge and you certainly should not jump into the middle of it and demand that it stop. That is not your role. Let the PMs and DMs do their job if they feel that it is going outside the boundaries that were established initially. You might also feel that someone in the community is being abused and want to rush to help them and be the "rescuer." That is not your judgment call either. Do NOT go up to him and insist that he is being abused and that it has to stop. This is not the time to be judgmental. What you can do is approach the individual in a friendly manner and say, "You know, I saw you doing some really hard things last time we were out. If you want to talk sometime don't hesitate to call if you need me." That way he will know that you are a compassionate person who is available if he needs you. Some people really get off on hard pain and that might be something you as a newbie are having a hard time getting your head around, but it is very attractive to those who enjoy it.

Integrity, honor and your reputation are all you really have in the public scene; you should safeguard these things.

Pitfalls

BDSM/kink can be a really hot and heavy engaging experience. After all, that is what attracts most of us to it! There has been a lot written and discussed about it as a sexually or physically centered activity, but it can also be incredibly powerful emotionally and mentally. In my experience there is something very special about being able to share kinky times with someone you love—but you may not be interested in love. However much humans love to fuck, sex usually comes with emotional and mental needs that may or may not be met by regular play partners. Not every situation is going to be perfect. What if your new submissive friend suddenly becomes so emotionally attached to you that she flies into a jealous rage if you discuss playing with someone else? How will you handle your feelings about your new Dominant who wants to create a stable of submissives? Should you feel hurt and left out? How will you feel if a scene comes to an end with both of you sweaty and exhausted on the floor, and you are just settling into a nice warm afterglow, and then your partner suddenly jumps up and says, "Hey, that was great but I have to get out of here!" and pulls on his or her pants and leaves?

People have their own needs and expectations, and how successfully you deal with negotiation before you play will help shape what is going to happen, and what might come apart in the end. Don't ask someone to provide something he or she cannot, and know what it is that you want. Know your own sexuality. If you have expectations that need to be met, then you have to initially ask if the other person can provide what you need. It is always better going in with both eyes open than having stars in them when that new Dominant meets your gaze across the room and your breath gets caught in your throat like a sparrow in a cage. You also don't want to heap all of your expectations on your partner. This is one of the reasons I caution people to have really explored their sexuality before they get too

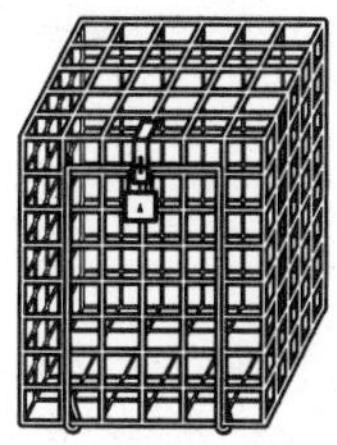

Your First Party

- ✔ Know your personal boundaries, know the play rules of the dungeon and identify the DM (Dungeon Master) in case he or she is needed.
- ✔ Don't touch what isn't yours unless invited—this goes for toys and people.
- ✔ Never interrupt a scene in progress at a party.
- ✔ Locate the cooldown area for après play and arrange a space in it for when you are done with your playmate.
- ✔ Be aware of which toys you have brought. (If you leave a toy at the end of the night, chances are you won't get it back, so leave the handcrafted floggers at home for personal enjoyment.)

wrapped up in kinky sex. You have to have the ability to enjoy an afternoon of delights and still be able to say, "That was lovely, I hope you have a great rest of the day," and then be able to leave and treasure the experience as a beautiful memory without any guilt or longing or jealousy. The tighter you hold on to something the faster you will lose it, and there are as many experiences to come as there are clouds in the sky. A lot of times people start playing with each other and they become regular partners outside of any sort of primary relationship. Emotions can and will develop with someone you play with; it is inevitable and sometimes it is reciprocal. You may love what someone does to you but you don't have to be in love with him or her. Recognize, validate and communicate that.

Karada: A body harness made of rope. Typically of Japanese origin; rope is tied around the body with diamond patterns descending down the body. Many practitioners of Japanese rope bondage (shibari) use it as a foundation for more complex ties.

If someone becomes too emotionally attached to you and you are uncomfortable, then you have to immediately take steps to reestablish boundaries. Immediately. Don't wimp out with the "If I just ignore them they will go away" method of dealing with situations—that is a terrible way to treat someone else. Be up front and honest. She may or may not like you afterward but she will respect you. This goes both for Dominants and submissives. Just because you like to be submissive doesn't mean you have to let yourself be blown in any direction someone else desires. Be a person with character and you will gain respect, and respect is very attractive.

Let me give you an example of how you might handle yourself in this situation: you have done all your reading, have about a year or two of experience under your belt and have become very well known for your flogging techniques that you show off at fetish parties. There is a very tasty sub that belongs to someone else and he or she comes up to you and asks you if you would be interested in playing with him. If you are also interested and you know he is "collared" (in a relationship involving belonging to or being owned by another) you should say thank you and then immediately turn to his Dominant/Mistress/Master/Top and say "Thank you for having X approach me. I would enjoy giving her a stout flogging; what are the boundaries you have both set?" Once you hear that, you can communicate your own boundaries. "So I can flog him here and there, no insertion, et cetera, and you do understand that I will not be providing any aftercare, yes?" This approach does something immediately—it automatically involves the sub's primary partner in the decision-making process. It asks him or her for her feedback and if she is a Dominant, she will respect your approach. It also reasserts her position as the Dominant in her relationship with the submissive. I hesitate to negotiate with a collared submissive on his or her own; I find the approach I've just described to be more proactive in dealing with boundaries. Always respect the boundaries you have been granted if you are playing with someone else's "toy."

Avoid situations that would have you playing on the side without a partner's notice; that can have a variety of endings and not many of them are good. Of course, this is assuming the situation involves a collared submissive or slave. What if someone is part of a slightly kinky couple but there are no roles defined? Take the same approach, just word it so it is softer and gentler. If you really are someone who is becoming known for your flogger technique then tell this sub nicely that you would like to take her up on her offer and "Let's go tell your partner, who is here tonight, all the yummy things I am going to do to you to warm you up for him later." Be open, honest and respectful and you will find your play-date calendar filling up quite quickly!

Chapter 6

Pain and Pleasure

What do we get out of being tied up, spanked, tortured and tormented? Where is the line between pleasure and pain and what are all the points in between? How do you determine where your own personal interest in sensation play lies and how do you know what is healthy "pain" and what is truly damaging? There are many lines and gray areas in kinky play, from a delicious bite on a nipple to a pair of snug clamps, to hard bondage and all points in between. What follows is meant to help you understand how we can experience pleasure from pain and how you may use it as a starting point for your kinky explorations.

Psychological and Physiological Characteristics of "Pain"

I like to think of "sensation play" as a large buffet dinner full of food that is varied and unique with its own flavors. Each one tastes a little different than the rest, each has its own texture and initial flavor and finish, and in combination with others it can produce even

Kennel Play: Part of Puppy Play, where the submissive or bottom is confined in a small dog kennel as part of the scene.

more intense and wonderful sensations. The title of this chapter is somewhat misleading; I find *pain* and *pleasure* to be somewhat limiting terms. It might better be titled Sensation Play. Those sensations are what will help release various chemicals and hormones in the body and create the experience of "flying" that people who reach "subspace" (which is just what it sounds like—more on this shortly) are always yammering on and on about. Don't be jealous if it hasn't happened for you yet. By helping you to understand it, I am going to give you a better chance getting there.

Are pain and pleasure opposites, or can they coexist in the same moment? Once I was getting a deep tissue massage. The therapist dug hard into my back and shoulders, pushing against the muscle so hard that the pain was excruciating. Then with a final push, the muscle reset back into its original position. There was a wave of euphoria accompanied by a deep, guttural moan reserved only for when I'm overwhelmed by sensation. It was as if someone had suddenly flipped a switch from intense pain to extraordinary pleasure. The change was sudden, but I was certainly not feeling pain and pleasure at the same time. I envy the "pain slut" masochists who take extreme pleasure in receiving uncomfortable sensations. To me, their ability to make pain and pleasure synonymous is as awe inspiring as it is foreign.

Like many bottoms, I endure pain for the eventual reward, but don't relish pain as the reward itself. I can remember being up against the St. Andrew's cross, my Top working over my all-too-sensitive nipples: digging into them with her sharp nails, clamping and twisting them to make me squirm and scream. Although I didn't find pleasure in the sensation itself, I did find it in my Top's gleeful response to my reactions. Another Top had me hold an uncomfortable position for a long period of time. She took pleasure in knowing that my muscles were burning, and knowing I was pleasing her kept me going. She was inspiring me to endure more pain in order to draw out that

Never underestimate the power that a slutty shoe holds. It embodies and embraces a woman's sexuality.

Leather Butt: A common term that describes a part of someone's body that has had prolonged stimulation, making that part less sensitive over time.

moment of mutual pleasure just a little bit longer. Tops need to be able to read their bottoms well. My tolerance for intense sensation will be different for each scene, depending on my mood, how tired I am, how often I've been playing, and other factors. The same cane stroke that left me squealing in pleasure last time could have me screaming in agony. After we've played a few times, Tops are able to read me a bit better. Of course, the easiest thing to do is just ask me how something feels. Once a Top can identify what's painful and what's pleasurable, he or she is able to dispense each in turn to orchestrate the scene.

—gregg, submissive extraordinaire

Lifestyle: Referring to involvement in BDSM *i.e.*, "How long have you been in the lifestyle?"

All play has to be within your personal limits. There is no point in suffering if you are getting nothing out of it; pain shouldn't exceed the receiver's hard limits, and this goes for Tops and bottoms, Doms and subs. Remember, this book is about getting into kinky sex for pleasure and gratification. We are talking about consensual "pain and pleasure"—although I have yet to meet a submissive or bottom who complains that there is too much *pleasure* and it is beyond his limits! There are bad types of pain such as the feeling of "pins and needles" in the hands and feet and this needs to be acknowledged as the circulatory system being restricted and the nerves letting you know that there is something wrong that requires immediate attention. If you feel a stabbing or numbness this too could be an indication of nerve pain or compression, and it is the body's way of telling you that there is something seriously not right. Nerve pain is not something to blow off casually. Beware of a play partner that encourages you to "suck it up" and "work through the pain" if it is this kind of pain! The types of pain we would like to deliver and have accepted are mostly musculoskeletal "pain," the delicious achy sensations that are desirable in BDSM. For instance, when I have a submissive tied up in a delicious and restrictive position and her muscles are groaning and achy from being bound, she relishes that enduring type of sensation. Now, if her hands or feet start to go numb and "fall asleep" that is a bad type of pain and has to be immediately addressed.

It takes a little practice to get to know your body, or that of your sub, and how it reacts to various toys and situations. When I was first starting out as a Dominant, I had a chance to meet a very lovely lass that I caught eyeing me up at a play party. We met, chatted and arranged for a playdate the following week at my place. She was also fairly new and we were immensely attracted to each other. I cleared my schedule, and we had an entire Saturday afternoon for exploring together. The first thing I did was tie her to my four-poster bed. I like to use a noncompressing type of "cuff" made out of rope for tying wrists and ankles and soon she was stretched on top of my eight-

Nowadays corsets have become more beautiful and elegant and are much more comfortable than those your grandmother wore.

hundred-thread-count duvet cover and looked delicious as the "damsel about to be in distress." Using a light deerskin flogger on her smooth belly and tender thighs, I was beginning to bring a nice flush to the skin, switching back and forth between nice, yummy and very safe slappy sensations to begin with, then adding harder striking that would make her jump a little. About fifteen minutes

1 Aim for the strong shoulder muscles or along the upper part of the rib cage.

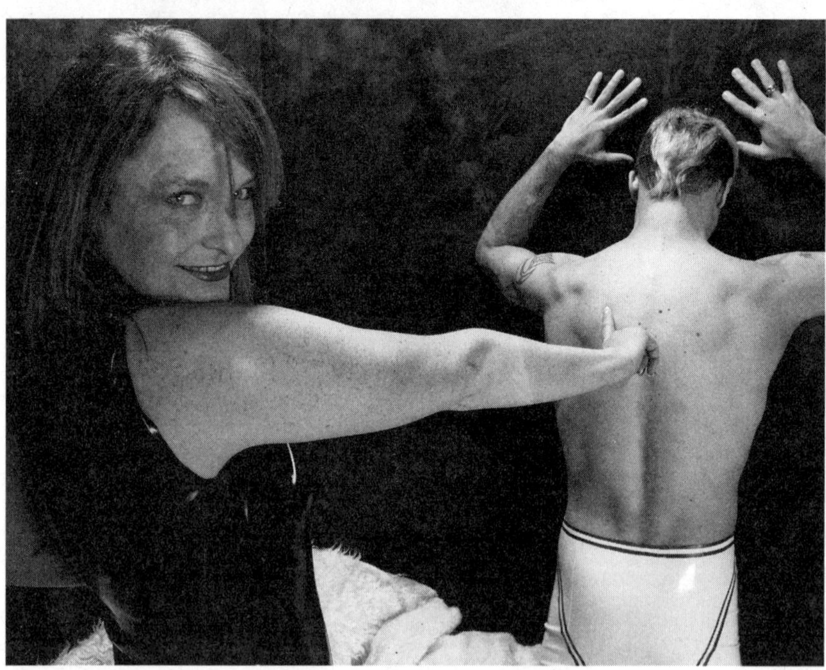

2 You want to be hit muscle, not the spine.

3 Alternate flogging the left and then the right half of the back.

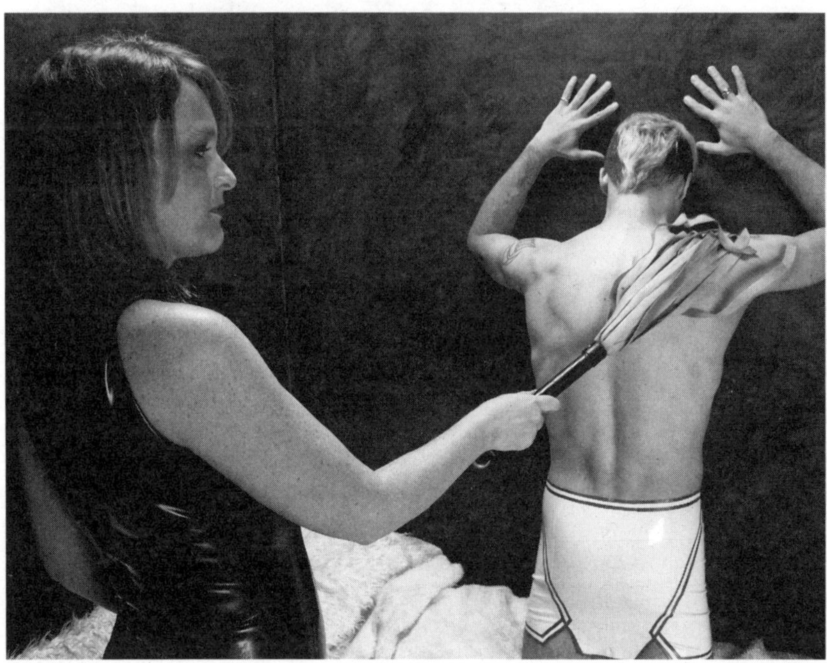

4 Enjoy!

Masochism: The act of receiving pain for sensual/ sexual pleasure.

into our playtime she looked at me and gently said, "Um, Sir, my fingers in my left hand are tingling." I replied, "Would you like the cuff off or just loosened?" Given a choice, she said "Please just loosen it a little; I am loving what you are doing." I checked her hands for circulation (see the thumbnail test in chapter 8) and it was apparent that in my eagerness I had tied her arms a little too tightly. It was a simple matter of loosening both restraints so she had about seven more inches of play in the rope, and that relieved her tingling sensations with the ability to flex her arms and wrists. A simple fix. Sometimes it can be a simple matter of readjusting the restraints or rearranging to make someone more comfortable in a realistic position. We were able to continue our scene without any other issues because we had previously negotiated that if there were any sensations that were of the "bad kind," she was to alert me and I would act upon it immediately.

> I am a submissive, but I don't have a desire to be collared. I am not about 24/7, just about having fun. What I get the most pleasure out of is bondage, really heavy bondage—immobilization. I love leather and metal together, it gets me really hot. However there needs to be an aesthetic beauty to what it is we are doing. I love heavy metal cuffs that are lined with leather. In my vanilla life I am really in control and play is a great therapeutic way of leaving my life behind for a few hours. I am not really into "pain" per se although there is a component of "challenge" that I enjoy immensely. I am bratty and can totally get my ass kicked for it during the scene, because I don't want to wimp out and afterward it feels like a badge of honor. I love to have my hair pulled, to be pushed around, picked up and manhandled roughly; even my bruises afterward have an aesthetic value that I enjoy, reminding me of my playdate for days afterward.
>
> —Jenica, submissive

Chances are you have surfed images on the Internet and seen hot pics of women and men bound in delicious and contorted

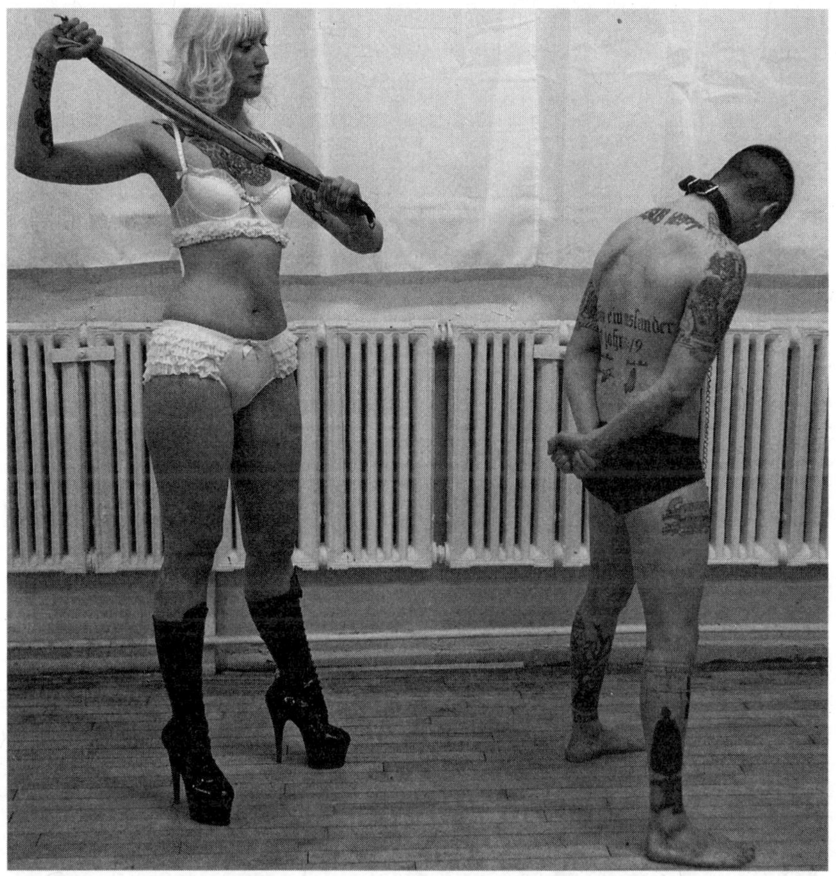

1 Stand your submissive up with his arms either crossed behind his back or outstretched on a wall or St. Andrew's Cross about four feet away from you. Tell him to remain still. Continues→

positions. Their torment looks deliciously exciting, their positions are hard-core looking and the torture intense but remember, this is the real world, and those are professional paid models. Reality can be just as hot, but it has to be more realistic and as a kinky person you need to understand the difference between the Internet and reality. Don't measure your own skills or evolution against those depicted in the media. You wouldn't judge yourself against a magazine ad or a movie star, so don't fall into the mind-set that every submission or domination experience should be just like what is depicted on the Internet. It won't be. It can't be.

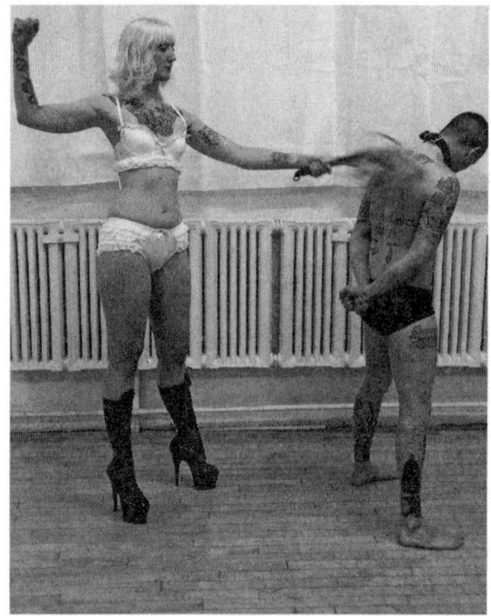

2 Grip the flogger handle with your dominant hand and gather the tails in your other hand. Notice how Freya's left and right arms are cocked and the tails of the flogger are as high as her head? This is called "potential energy."

3 In one motion, quickly move the hand holding the handle forward and let go of the tails. Aim for the shoulders, not for the spine or the kidneys. This is the "kinetic energy" because it is moving.

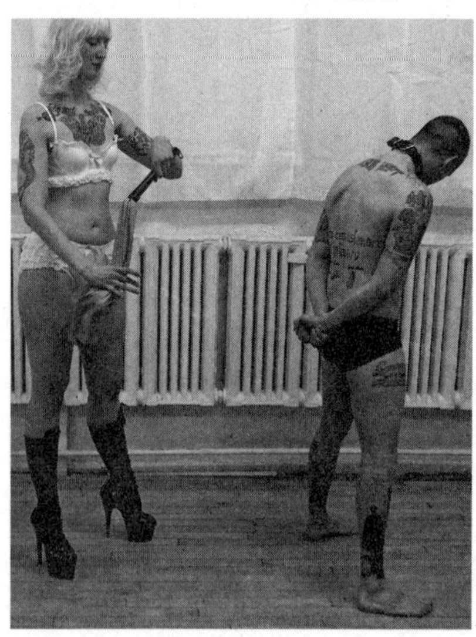

4 Once it strikes, let the tails fall downward.

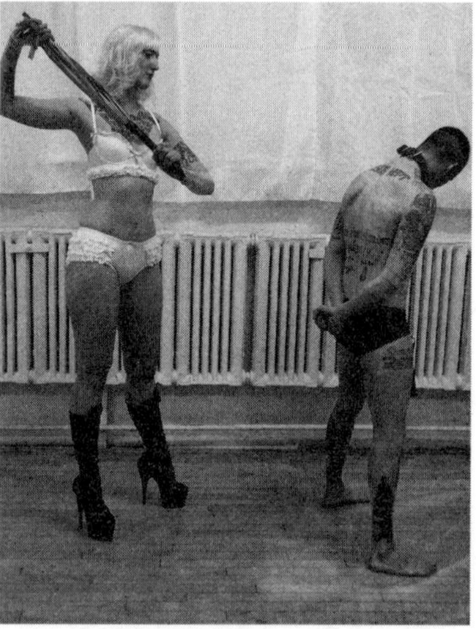

5 In a sweeping motion gather up the tails and return to position 1, ready to repeat. This is called the "follow through."

It can be better.

Better to have a partner you care about and can really get intimate with and explore all those nooks and crannies in both of your psyches. To find out what turns someone on immensely and then take her on a delicious journey; to push his limits and embrace him afterward in your arms and hold him close. To see them endure all of your torment just for the simple fact that they care about enduring for you and your ministrations. The ideal submissives want to endure and persevere "just because" as their Dominant it pleases you to see them suffer deliciously. And then when it is all over and you are both feeling that exquisite afterglow of satisfaction and connectedness, the experience is much more rewarding than the cold circuitry of servers, keyboards or the corporate product of fetish porn could ever be.

Master: Dominant male in a BDSM relationship. Also implies they are masters of their area of expertise.

Pleasure. I love that word. I love the aspect of controlling a woman's feelings, her reactions and ultimately her orgasm. I love to seduce; I am very tactile and take pleasurable touch to a whole other level. I might start with a simple massage or back rub and a long foot massage as well. If people can get over the barrier of touch, it can break down the walls that deter really deep communication. For myself I am more intuitively able to communicate thorough touch than through conversation. I see it as its own language—I can convey confidence without ever saying a word. I love the erotic, sensual horniness that you can feel from your partners when you are in tune with them. The other half of the journey is the response I get from them. Noticing how they react when I get near their erogenous zones, how breathing quickens. It is a dead giveaway and they don't have to say a word for me to understand where they are and where they are going and that I am going to take them there.

For example, I had a beautiful woman facedown on my carpet and was straddling her bum. After I had massaged her for a while, I had her raise herself up on her forearms so I could

Milking: Stimulating a male's prostate with a finger or dildo to produce an orgasm. Also refers to causing him to orgasm repeatedly until he is unable to produce any more ejaculate. A nap afterward is inevitable.

firmly but gently stroke her as I slipped my hands under her sweater to cup her engorged nipples and the soft fullness of each breast. Her body language and moans directed me to understand without speaking a word that she would like me to go further. The suggestion is made via touch, and the response is the indication of how turned on she is and because there are very few words spoken it takes things to a more primal, carnal level for us both where words aren't necessary.

—Cristophe, Top

Playing can be very physical. I highly recommend that bottoms or submissives practice yoga or some form of exercise routine that focuses on stretching, as well as living a healthy lifestyle. As a bottom you will take a lot of physical intensity from the Top or Dominant and you should take care of your body and fine tune your relationship with it. It is the only one you have; keep it happy before we make it ache and groan. This attitude also goes for your play partners—you want someone who will respect your body as well. There is a classic saying in the kink world: if you break your toys, you don't get to play with them again. This goes for partners as well as other toys. Tops *and* bottoms should take this to heart.

Subspace

Subspace: what is this mythical creature that you keep hearing bandied about on the Internet and in books? It is a wonderful combination of the right moment in a scene, the right sensations, the right ambience and the resultant endorphins that give a submissive or bottom the sensation of leaving his or her body or "flying." It doesn't happen all the time, but when it does it makes kinky sex a magical experience. How do you get there? Achieving this state is usually the result of many variables, one of them being how intense a sensation is. Pain is a sensation but so is pleasure. Using sensation to take someone on an exquisite journey is exciting and exhilarating. Not many people can orgasm just by sheer pain alone. If you as a Dominant concentrate just on administering pain as a sensation

Local dungeon spaces sometimes rent their rooms for couples to play in. Don't be shy to ask around, high-quality bondage equipment is a delight to play on.

Mistress: Dominant female in a BDSM relationship. Also implies they are masters in their area of expertise.

then you are really missing out on a wide variety of sensations available for this journey. The same goes for pleasure. The journey between both sensations is what keeps playtime interesting and special, varying the sub's experience and giving his mind and body time to absorb and process it. Typically the body can get used to almost any sensation after about twenty minutes; then the receptors in the body read it all as about "the same" and work at blocking it out. Think about it this way: You can deliver a long, luxurious massage, during which your partner is putty under the firm strokes of your hands. He or she feels all yummy and warm, but wouldn't it be a

Munch: A casual gathering of people who are into BDSM meeting at a vanilla place (such as a pub) for friendly socializing. There is no play or showing off of toys (including people) at a Munch.

nice way to accentuate those feelings if your blood-red nails were sharply toying with his nipples? How about the same massage, but your partner is blindfolded and each time you slide your hands over her body, the hair on her skin stands up to attention and her breathing increases, and then you dangle a few hot drips of wax and splash them onto her belly? That sharpness will make her crave the yummy sensations even more! Building and working a nice ebb and flow between yummy feelings and intense ones, and how creatively you execute that journey is what will set you apart from the

Sometimes all the outfit a woman needs is a pair of slutty boots.

average, run-of-the-mill Top. Think of your playmate's body as a beautiful musical instrument intended for your enjoyment. Would you rather play a symphony with it or produce the kind of tinny sound that squawks from an AM radio? How much is your sexuality worth? Don't you want the best for both of you?

Mummification: A type of bondage where the submissive is wrapped completely with plastic wrap, duct tape or fabric. Caution: close monitoring is important as the body can overheat quickly when completely wrapped.

> I lie on a table, blindfolded and waiting. Sir has wrapped my body with so much rope I feel like a fly ready to be cast as bait. And bait I am. Lips touch my mouth, soft, but not Sir's. A rush of warmth and anticipation floods down my body; Sir has opened the door, I am a free-for-all. I will not disappoint Sir; I return the kiss with enthusiasm. Something soft touches between my legs. A hand? Feathers? Another set of lips press against mine. The coarse fibers of the hemp rope bite into my skin as I writhe in delight at being so exposed. My blindfold keeps me in solitude, but I am the helpless center of attention.
>
> —Haba, submissive

Together you can both get to that space of interconnectedness where time and feelings melt into the moment if you take your time and try not to have expectations that you "need" or "should" get there. Learning about your partner and what gets him or her off is all about caring for him and not every scene has to be hard hitting with a heavy flogger or whip—it is really good to be creative and explore all the subtle nuances of his sexuality. Maybe he likes to be tied up and tickled. Maybe she just wants to be bound and gagged and left alone in some quiet time. Maybe she wants a DP with you and that new toy you brought home, or maybe she's having an illicit affair with the Hitachi Magic Wand and wants you to use it more on her. It doesn't matter what takes your partner there; what matters is that YOU are the one taking him there. There is never any reason to be jealous of or see yourself as "competing" with toys, what is important is that YOU are wielding them and being a connected partner. Being in the moment with your playmate, trading feelings and intimacy is what's important. Everything else is just a

Negotiation: Coming to an agreeable arrangement based on activities and interests.

tool. If you aren't feeling "it" on a particular evening and your partner is, you can either say "Not tonight, baby" or perhaps just doing a nice simple hog-tie and letting her lie at your feet while you read the paper is a compromise both of you can live with. I find that in kinky sex there are so many varying degrees of excitement that something simple that doesn't require a large exertion of effort can be a way of saying "I am not feeling up for a big scene but I still care about you, now open your mouth and let me put the ball gag in so I don't have to listen to you whine anymore." It all depends on your level of involvement with your partner; all of this is only as "real" as you want to make it.

Him

I don't see myself as a sadist who likes to hurt people, but I do enjoy inflicting pain. To see the way the human body reacts to a pinch or a slap or the crack of a whip is fascinating, and to see the pleasure my lovely wife, cat, gets from it is truly a thrill. Everyone has a different level of pain tolerance. I like to push a person to that level and have her want more. I get excited when my wife becomes animalistic and completely oblivious to the world around her when I've whipped her with a flogger. The raw sexual energy that it creates in her gets passed to me, driving us to levels I never thought possible. Feeling her skin tensing and trembling under my touch, knowing she's wondering "Will it hurt? How much will it hurt? How long will it hurt?" is my one true mental sadistic quality—making her wonder just what I'm going to do to her next.

—Rat, Dominant

Her

The warmth and wholeness I feel while being in a masochistic role is hard to explain to those that haven't experienced it before. Coming into a play session I feel younger and shyer than I have in years. Then during the application and receiving of pain I feel warmth, happiness, confidence, strength,

1 Arm sleeves are very sexy and can make your partner beautifully helpless.

Continues→

2 Unzip the sleeve and have him straighten his arms behind his back.

3 Slide the sleeve up the arms, taking care not to do any sudden, jerky movements.

control and beauty. With the rush of endorphins I can understand how I can feel some of these things. The others I like to think I feel because I am growing and learning, strengthening a hidden side of myself that shows in my daily routines.

The physical attributes like slimming and tightening of the skin, toning of the muscles, and cardio advantages of course give me another reason to love it. My husband, Rat, a sadist and percussionist, inflicts the pain play upon me. When we are together in these roles I feel a closer bond with him than in any of our fifteen years together. Consensual pain is as gratifying as most sexual encounters. We breathe as one, think as one, climax as one, love as one. —cat, submissive

In my experience, when I go to a playdate with the expectation of something specific happening—say, a woman squirting or letting me try out a new way of tying her to the bed/coffee

4 Take the first strap and run it diagonally across the chest.

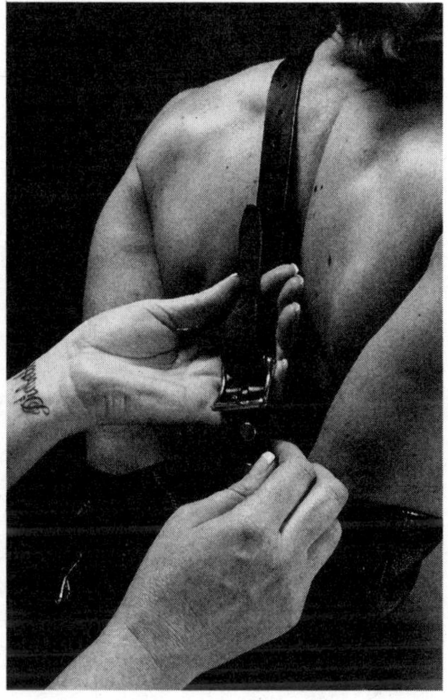

5 Fish it through the buckle. Take care not to put too much strain on the shoulder joints. Continues→

table/kitchen island—and it doesn't happen, then it's a problem with my own expectations and not any fault of hers. You have to let go of the desire to force something; enjoy it if it does happen and don't dwell on it if it doesn't. No individual is quite the same, and what worked for one person won't necessarily work for another. Letting go of expectations, getting lost in the moment, and seeing where the scene goes is one of the beautiful aspects of kinky sex. Enjoy the journey. Many times I might have riding crops and candles at the ready, but instead of my tying her tightly to the bed, she moans when I clasp her wrists together in my large palm and pin them helplessly above her head while I trace and tease her pouting lips with a strawberry, left over from dessert, held gently in my own. I avoid scripted scenes. I like to have a general idea of what I would like to explore based on my partner's own responses and desires and I always keep that in my head, but I hesitate to force something that isn't working. How

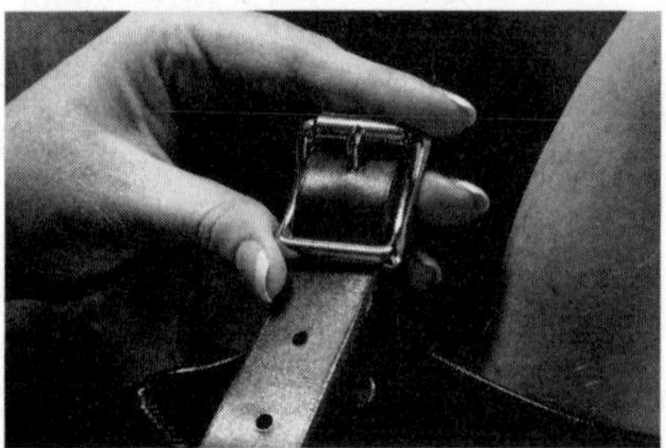

6 Buckle it and repeat with the other strap.

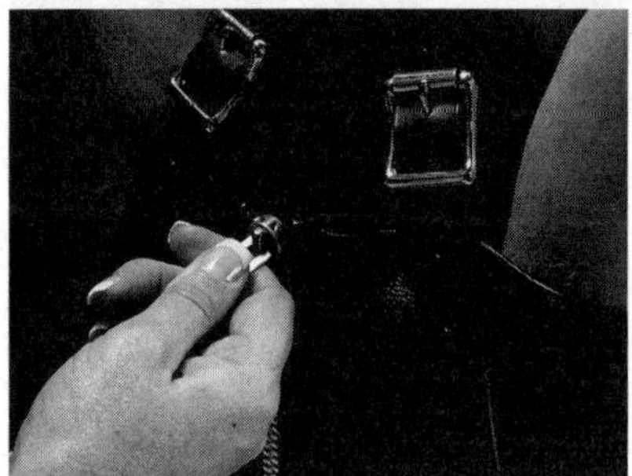

7 Zip it up gently; you want to give your submissive's arms the chance to get used to it.

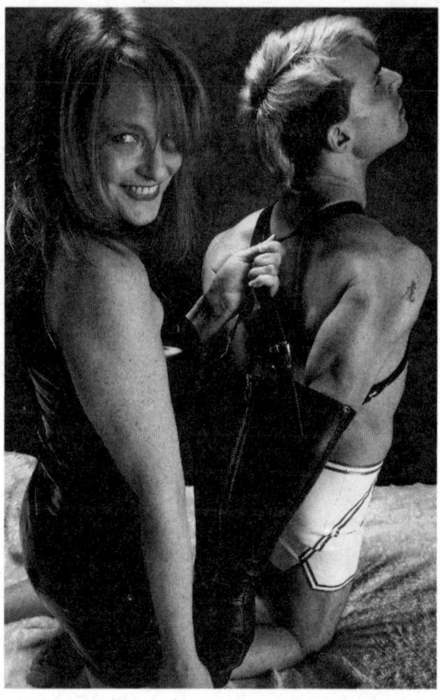

8 Hang on to the straps and force him around where you want to.

things go can also be affected by the type of day the other person is having, if they are tired or well rested, or even if he or she has had enough to eat. Some people find that it is either harder or easier to get to subspace depending on their experience levels. Someone who is an experienced bottom may understand the nuances of his body so well that he knows his triggers and what will help him get to subspace.

> I have a control issue. I am always in control—at work, in my home life, et cetera—and when I am going to play with someone I embrace the submissive side of me and allow them to take over the reins. There is a release where I can yell and scream and yelp and cry and then still be able to take more. I love to push myself and I hate to fail. If someone who is playing with me uses the term "you are being punished" I actually get upset. I respond very well and can push my limits if instead they are

encouraging and supportive. When I go into a scene with someone I start by asking myself "What is going to test my limit today?" I enjoy a thuddy type of pain, not so much the sharp and stingy, but it also depends on my feelings that day and how far I want to push myself. As far as pleasure goes, I love the exquisiteness of a good mind fuck. If I am blindfolded, my mind cycles through all the possibilities. What are they picking up to hit me with next? How are they looking at me? What are they thinking of next? I find that very pleasurable—the anticipation.

—Tracy, submissive

Newbie (or Noob): Slang term for someone new to BDSM. Can be an endearing term.

The Dominant sets the stage for the submissive to explore him or her self. Doms are merely the vehicle by which their playmates investigate their own boundaries. Context is key. The Dom gets to play god, the puppet master, the one that controls everything about the scene and the stimuli that the sub is being tormented or rewarded with. Everything is based upon a foundation of trust, and trust is what makes or breaks a scene. Whether you are going to administer a harsh sensation or a yummy one, having your partner submit and surrender to it carries an amazing sexual charge.

Pain, in varying forms, is an integral aspect of our Domination/submission relationship. Erotic pain, pleasurable pain, and the extreme pain involved in punishment, are each woven into the fabric of our life partnership. As different as each is, they all give me, the Dominant, pleasure. I enjoy meting out physical pain and what builds before it is even more intoxicating. That is anticipation. Anticipation, the rising excitement flowing from knowing that a scene will happen at a specified time. For the Dominant, the anticipation is in the planning; for the submissive, the anticipation is in the suspense of not knowing just how the scene might unfold. Although we enjoy vanilla sex regularly, the heightened eroticism of kinky sex is often the best. The anticipation can begin with simple directions such as "no panties" when we dine out, or with an action; having my

Objectification: Play in which one person is put on display or dehumanized as part of sexual play.

sub enter a café for takeout while naked under her coat is a favorite of mine. Her instructions for preparation can be a little more involved: dressing in the specified lingerie, putting a blindfold on, and kneeling at the door holding a glass of wine in anticipation of my return. Another favorite game is "Implement of the Day." I speak those words in the morning and she is left wondering all day what implement will be hanging inside the front door when she returns from work. Upon arrival, she wordlessly takes the implement upstairs, undresses, bathes, shaves herself and lies naked on the bed awaiting my arrival. Our erotic play usually begins with percussion: spanking, paddling, light cropping or caning. Cuddling, kissing, and caressing follow, interspersed with pussy whipping, and clitoral or nipple torture. The goal is to integrate the pain with the eroticism until she is on the edge of an orgasm. She must ask permission to orgasm; it can be denied or delayed until I grant permission.

—Master William, Dominant

Submissives, slaves, bottoms and usually Switches will all tell you what their "cage" looks like. In other words, what makes them tick, what makes them horny and wet and stiff and hard, how they like to be treated and what makes them crave playtime. All a Dominant or Top has to do is listen and listen carefully. I have been accused of being "scary" at times as a Dominant "because you listen, Morpheous, and not many do." That is possibly the most important wisdom I can offer. Listen. Really listen to what your playmates are saying. They absolutely will tell you how big their cage is, where the bars are and where their escape routes are; where the restraints are, how they like to be tied and where their interests lie that will make them crave to go back into that cage again and again. Your role as a Dominant or Top is to facilitate their journey and keep them in their cage so they can better explore their own desires and experiences. Consensually, of course.

Throughout this book I have stressed communication, the

ability to really listen and process what it is your partner desires and how you can best tie your own desires to those. It is one thing to be a "service Top" but it is another to be able to marry your own needs and desires with your bottom's. A Top has to be able to communicate his or her needs as well; this isn't a one-way street—any dance of sexuality requires both partners playing their roles and relishing them. One person can lead and the other follow but they both are twirling on the same dance floor.

Odalisque: Old Skool term for a female sex slave.

A bad schoolgirl is always in trouble with the Dean.

Oreo Model: Sandwiching a challenging aspect of a given situation between two positive points during a discussion.

As an adolescent I suffered from a not unpleasant affliction of vivid fantasies. I would spend hours lost in a dreamworld that consisted of dark reveries where I could withstand and apply great violence, garnished by exhilarating sexual stimulation. It did not take long to realize that this was a characteristic that the majority of my peers could not identify with, and so I learned at an early age to keep my lurid daydreams to myself. As I moved into young adulthood I began to be aware of a subculture that caters to taboo affinities, where dark fantasies are realized into a reality, accompanied with strict borders of consent between all participants, with a firm grasp on margins of safety. At first my awareness came in the form of books, Internet sites and workshops. Through these mediums I came into contact with a Dominant who readily spotted my eagerness and offered to gratify longings of mine that had remained buried for many years.

I accepted his offer to create a scene with him, based entirely upon my own desires. He encouraged me to speak of things that until then had largely remained unspoken. I admitted to my cravings for receiving a whipping; to be restrained and given lashes in a manner reminiscent of punishment among seafaring men who had lived centuries ago. To my delight I was finally put within the constraints of an old and deep desire! Tied and pressed against a one-hundred-year-old wooden post in his loft, I placed myself at his mercy, with my tender nipples rubbing against the raw wood while he whipped my naked ass and thighs. To be in a position I had only dreamed of was a pleasure for which words cannot do justice. The raw pain was exhilarating, refreshing, new and terribly welcome. The responses of my body under such inflicted pain were a marvel; to experience it is to experience yourself, to understand your boundaries in a way that is unique and intimate between the sufferer and the inflictor.

This experience was my rebirth in a sense, giving me a new perception of my body and its wide range of sensation. I feel privileged to have the ability to undergo intense pain and come

Many submissives feel a sense of peace when they experience subspace.

> out of it feeling refreshed, rejoicing in the awareness of my body's personal responses. I have finally gained the understanding that all parts of me are valid, that every dark urge can be realized, that enjoyment of pain can be accepted; and I have reached a new heightened sense of reality.
>
> —Sabrina, submissive

Sub and Top Drop

Equally as important as subspace are sub drop and top drop. Either of these can occur anywhere from immediately after play, to hours or days after an intense play session. It can manifest itself in a variety of ways, mostly as feelings of depression, withdrawal, anger or a violent reaction against what it is the kinky player has either let herself do or have done to her. In an intense scene, a Dominant is opening up the bottom or submissive emotionally as well as physically and mentally. Again, trust is the most precious trait we have when we play with kinky sex. There

1 When spanking be sure to hit the juicy, fleshy parts of their bottom.

can be emotional valleys and peaks and these can tend to sweep over the person within forty-eight hours of a scene. He or she may feel devalued or worthless and oftentimes may have a hard time reconciling what they have been involved with. This is one of the reasons you should only play with people that have established boundaries and are effective at communicating them.

Sub drop can most certainly manifest as crying, and the sub may even unilaterally decide that he or she should leave the situation. The Top or Dominant needs to BE THERE for the sub. If you are going to take someone on a journey into subspace, where he or she is going to experience a wide variety of sensations, then you have the responsibility to make sure that individual "returns to earth" after his or her trip is done. Failure to do so demonstrates a lack of character. It isn't easy being the Dominant, we have to have one foot grounded in reality, and we set up the scene and take the other per-

2 Not on the tailbone or the small of their back.

Continues→

son through it inch by delicious inch. Submissives endure all the creative and devilish things we have concocted for them and they absolutely need someone to be there for them when they are done with their trip. This person is most likely you; however, more experienced players may go back to their primary partners for succor, or may simply understand better how to cope with what they might be going through mentally or physically. I ALWAYS have a new partner call me the next day to check in and see if there is anything that is required of me.

How do you address the situation if your play partner is having a nasty sub drop? You treat her like the special person she is. She has just allowed you to play a symphony with her body and mind and now you are going to hold her and reassure her during the cooldown period. I highly recommend a cooldown period, during which you go off somewhere else (if at a play party) out of

3 Start off gently with nice even whacks with the paddle and then build the intensity.

the center of attention, and snuggle and hold your partner. If he or she doesn't want to have physical contact then bring him some water, and be the compassionate person you are. He might be confused and anxious and need reassurance that he is okay and you will be there for him. Talking helps a lot; sharing past experiences and how you both dealt with them can help a bottom or submissive reground herself.

What isn't discussed much is the subject of top drop, which doesn't usually manifest itself as visually as crying, but commonly involves feelings of emptiness and being alone. Tops and Dominants don't usually discuss it because, hey, we're always in control—right?—but just as submissives need us, we need others for support as well. Humans are social creatures and Tops need a social framework that will support them. I had one such personal experience a number of years ago at a weekend-long retreat with a lot of my kinky friends. It was in the woods at a campground, and I spent all weekend long tying up pretty girls for their Tops and Dominants, and having a lot of fun doing it. I was single and still new to the community and I felt flattered that so many people wanted me to tie up their partners, as I was emerging as a new rope bondage artist. Top drop didn't hit me until the last night of the event. I had played pretty hard and was winding up with some quiet time in the pool around midnight. There were storm clouds rolling in the distance, some stars blanketing the sky above me and I was floating in the pool at the campground all alone with the sounds of play and laughter and music in the distance. All of a sudden I felt incredibly alone. I felt like the water I was floating in was washing over me and draining me of my energy. I started thinking of all of the other times I had found myself alone and this was a shocking revelation to me as I had never had a wave of loneliness hit me this strongly before. I am a very independent person; I enjoy world travel and have spent long times in solitude when traveling, but I had never felt this lonely in my entire life.

Recognizing that there must be some correlation with the activities I had been involved in all weekend long, I explored the threads of what I was feeling and why. After reflection for a little while I did the best thing I could do at a time like this—I got out of the pool and went and found my friends. I knew that the best remedy for my feelings would be to seek out my support structure—my friends—and be with them. I wasn't in a place where I couldn't think logically by any means, I just needed to be around people, and I had never heard of top drop. Still I realized what was happening had to be related to what happens to submissives and bottoms when they drop. You don't have to be an island—if you need help, ask for it. If you need to be around people, ask them or just go to where they are. You don't always have to verbalize what it is you are going through, your

Five Things About "Pain"

- ✔ Take time to warm up their body before going hard.
- ✔ Good "pain" is delicious and achy.
- ✔ Bad Pain is a stabbing or numbness.
- ✔ You don't have to get to subspace every time.
- ✔ Abuse is when the power dynamic is nonconsensual.

Orgasm Denial: When the Dom/me does not permit the submissive to reach orgasm without permission. Can be coupled with making them have sex or perform sex acts while simultaneously denying them an orgasm.

friends will understand. You aren't alone and there is no reason you should be—Tops and bottoms alike.

Abuse

How do you determine what is play and what is abuse? People who play with BDSM can easily be misinterpreted by those not understanding of the dynamic. If you were at the gym and you saw someone in the changing room with bruises and welts all over his or her backside you might be horrified to think that their partner or spouse was responsible. But if you were at the Friday night party where he or she received those welts you might have fond memories of a really great time of consensual activities between that individual and her Dominant. I keep mentioning *consent* as it is key to all kinky play. But what if you feel someone, or yourself, is in an abusive situation—how can you tell? Granted the lines can be blurred at times, but here are a few signs of actual abuse and they can be found in much more detail on the Internet and other publications listed in the back of this book. But for now ask yourself the following questions.

Abuse is when the dynamic is not consensual. Does the person's partner constantly put him or her down or exhibit extremely controlling behavior in front of others without the person's consent? Is the partner extremely jealous and jumps to conclusions or makes accusations? Does the person become very shy or timid around his or her partner? Has she withdrawn from family and friends? Does he suddenly cancel plans at the last minute? Are her finances controlled by the dominanting partner? Does she have unexplained marks or bruises?

Some of this walks a very gray line between BDSM and the vanilla world. What happens at a play party on a Saturday night could easily be misinterpreted as abuse to outsiders who are peering in and don't understand what kinky play can encompass. **One clear key sign that abuse is abuse is when the power dynamic is nonconsensual.**

What can you do if you think someone is being taken advantage of and suffering from abuse? You can be supportive and offer shelter. But the individual has to want help. You cannot make someone leave a situation no matter how hard you try and cajole or convince them. I know it is difficult to see someone you care about suffer, but he or she has to ask for help. It is not your role to make life decisions for others; they may be involved in a complex dynamic by their own consent—but if they aren't and if they DO ask for help then you can give them shelter and assistance, and put them in touch with a therapist immediately. In the scene we have seen the rise of kink-friendly therapists and doctors over the past few years, people that are educated about the distinction between kinky dynamics and what constitutes abuse. They are professionals that can help your friend or loved one much more than you can and they should be sought out. What you shouldn't do is stage an intervention, especially if you are untrained in such situations. People have to ASK for help. Do not make decisions for them. Be supportive and be their friend and let them know your door is open 24/7 if they need you. Oftentimes the knowledge that there is a support system can be key to such individuals seeking assistance.

Chapter 7

Kink in Toyland

A big part of kinky sex is fetishizing your toy collection. Sometimes you will buy a toy and it will be as great as you thought, and other times it won't quite live up to your expectations. You might buy a dildo with a little rabbit on the end of the thingy that is supposed to stimulate your—or her—clit and find it doesn't provide quite as much intensity as you might like, and then try the dildo with the beads in it and love it! Personal preference is everything, so get to know your body and what it likes. It doesn't matter if the toy is store bought or improvised at home, all that matters is that it works for you.

Part of the fun with toys is exploring with them in unconventional ways—for instance, what if you put the dildo in the freezer for a while before playing with it? Likewise, dropping it in a bowl of hot water can make for new sensations. Don't microwave it, though, or you'll find a big misshapen dildo when you are done and be left with a weird smell in the microwave that you will have a hard time getting rid of. I eventually had to throw my microwave

Two different types of leather collars showing the tri-ring and single ring.

Orientation Play: When a partner is instructed to participate in sexual activity or touching with another person that contradicts their natural sexual orientation. Can be part of Humiliation play.

out after making this mistake! Saran Wrap isn't just for leftovers anymore. Plastic wrap is a very quick way to immobilize someone without the nasty side effect of duct tape, which, when it comes off, will peel your body hair like skin from a banana.

Make Your Own

You don't have to have a lot of money to get off—humans have been getting off for longer than corporate sex toy manufactures have been around. If you have a chance to take in the sex museums in New York City and Amsterdam you can see some of the displays that trace the evolution of sex toys. I have a certain fondness for early-nineteenth-century erotic objects created around the beginning of the industrial revolution; the kinkiness of the toys being used in such a rigidly moral society makes me smile, especially when so much time and care must have been put into their creation in private. I also love the quack medical tools for which we have found pleasurable new uses, such as the Violet Wand. One hundred years ago it was used to assist with electrotherapy and now it is a toy that you might see at a fetish event or private dungeon making pretty girls and boys jump!

Humans are so adaptable as toolmaking creatures that we can and will improvise toys out of seemingly innocuous things. Ask yourself this: what is it I want to do? Then look around for

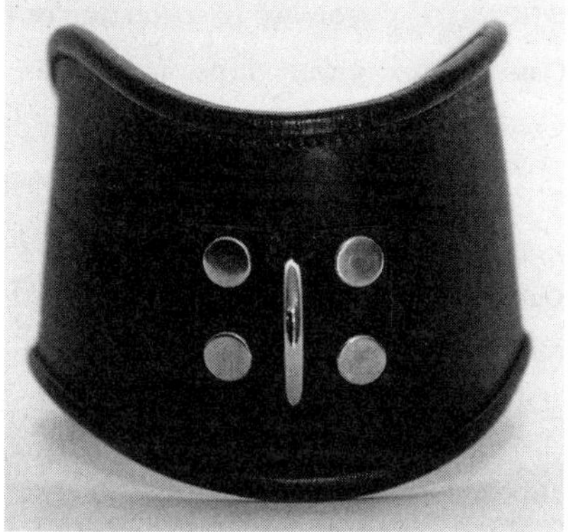

Back and front of a Posture Collar, which keeps a person's chin up and restricts movement.

objects to create that sensation. Do you want something percussive? How about something snappy or prickly? Perhaps something soft and sensual? It's all about the sensations you want to give or receive; let your mind get creative!

> Lots of things get me hot. If I am alone and I am turned on I usually take out my trusty pink dildo. I've experimented with pretty much anything I could find around the house: hairbrush handles, cucumbers, carrots. I haven't found anything I like more than my dildo or a real cock inside of me but the experimentation is a lot of fun, including improvising with things found at dollar stores. It's amazing what you can improvise with for insertive play. I make sure it is smooth and comfortable with no sharp edges and if I am concerned with how clean it is I will even put a condom on it just for an extra layer of protection.
>
> —Stephie, bottom

Why spend five hundred dollars on a buttery leather flogger with a jeweled handle that is personally weighted to your own specifications if you don't have to? Obviously that expensive flogger is a pretty yummy experience in terms of fetishizing toys purely for selfish reasons. Lots of kinky people fetishize equipment because it is fun and selfish. Deliciously selfish. But when

OTK: Classic position for spanking—Over the Knee.

Outing: Compromising someone's personal space or kinky lifestyle non-consensually by announcing either their orientation or interests to others. NOT allowed.

you are first starting out, you need to try a number of toys—floggers, whips, canes, crops, gags, et cetera, to find out what YOU like. Price can make a difference, but not in every case, especially if a craftsperson or artisan is just starting out and becoming established. Imagine if you had been able to meet some of the world-famous whip-makers of today fifteen or twenty years ago when they were still becoming established craftspeople. Wouldn't you love to own a Michael Murphy whip from back in the day? He is an exceptional Australian whip-maker of world renown (check out Murphywhips.com). Today there are lots of craftspeople that are still becoming established and I highly encourage you to support them so they can go on to become the Michael Murphys of the next generation. There have been more and more "kinky craft shows" popping up over the years that have become bigger and bigger. This gives both new and established artisans who are dedicated to the art and skill of their particular craft the chance to show off their wares and meet people face-to-face and show them how much time and effort go into each piece. If you go to larger leather conventions you will find just as many things for sale from individual artisans and if you buy something you can get that warm feeling in your tummy knowing you helped support someone who needs it. Not quite as warm as your partner's ass is going to be when you use that new paddle tonight, but you get the idea.

When I was finishing up my undergraduate degree I was one of those craftspeople trying to share my skill level and talent with the world, making exotic wooden paddles. Woods deeply nut colored such as cocobolo from Brazil, bright yellow canary wood and pink ivory from Africa, vibrant orange padauk from Southeast Asia and others were shaped into exquisite spanking implements. I put a lot of time and effort into these, finishing them with a non-toxic hand-oiled finish to bring out the beauty of the wood, each one designed to be a little different from the next so that each was truly as unique and individual as the person who bought it. I sold them at kinky craft shows and a few shops in Toronto and of course via email. Business got good enough that I was able to pay my rent for the last six months of my first degree by way of kinky people supporting my work, and for that I was truly thankful. In return those people that did purchase one of my Crimson Paddles supported a new artisan and now have a toy for life. Hang on to them—they are collector's items now as there will never be any more produced!

Flogging and whipping implements certainly are the first toys that conjure up images of kinky play and they are strong contenders for the most popular BDSM toys, but so many other sensations can be created from simple, everyday objects. We have five senses—use them! Olfactory play, as well as using flavors, can add an extra dimension to your lovemaking. For now, let's look at the basic PBS.

Painslut: A person who enjoys receiving a heavy degree of pain but may or may not enjoy submitting. They are more interested in the sensation rather than the mental aspects of submitting.

Penetration

What could be hotter than penetrating someone? Penetrating them repeatedly of course! There is something incredibly intimate in using a toy or yourself to penetrate another person in a safe and caring way. To have them open themselves up to you in a vulnerable position, emotionally, mentally and physically, shows great care and trust. Cherish the trust.

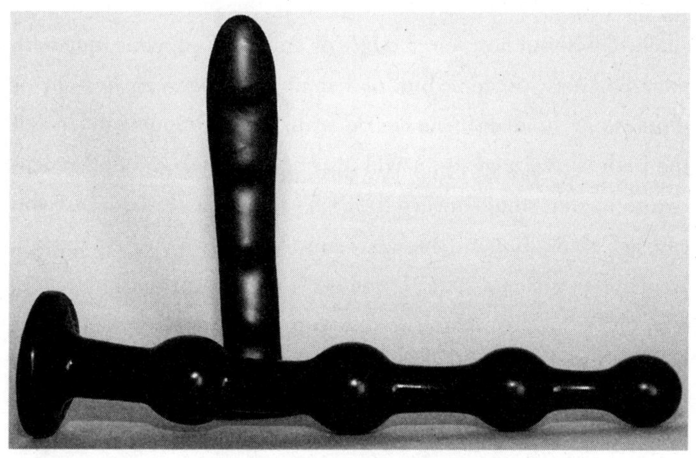

Silicone anal beads (front) and ribbed silicone dildo (back).

> It [penetration] is the most literal, physical form of sexual domination, the initial giving way; like, you are a little tight, and there is something so incredible in that first moment of penetration, and then the whole time it is this kind of back and forth, and just when you think it can't get much better it does. For me there is nothing better than feeling "full." The absolute feeling of surrender when somebody is pushing down on you with all their weight, and you can feel the warmth passing from their chest into yours. With a toy, it is a good, but different feeling. More exotic. I love good old-fashioned human penetration more than anything, but I probably get the most wet with a toy. It is nice because it offers more variety and has an element of voyeurism to it; he can sit back and watch everything that it is doing to me.
>
> —Alaris, Switch

A vagina can take a lot; after all, a baby can come through there, but that isn't to say you can jump in with both feet without any warm-up. Some people love being penetrated by fingers and toes; others like fists; still others love dildos, vibrators and "pervertable" objects like vegetables and hairbrush handles. What is most important is that anything going into someone, whether via the bum or the vagina or the mouth, needs to be smooth, without any rough edges or ends. Taking your time with your partner, warming him or her up, playing with her clit or nipples or whatever turns her on is absolutely important, since if the body is warmed up, it will also be more relaxed and receptive to having things inserted. It isn't a race to see how fast you can get something in there, or how big it can be. Not at all. Remember this is a special moment you are sharing with someone: either you are going to put something inside your partner or you are inviting him to put something inside you. Forget about porn images you have seen, relax and be in the moment. It is your body and learning about what can and can't go in "there" is part of learning about kinky sex.

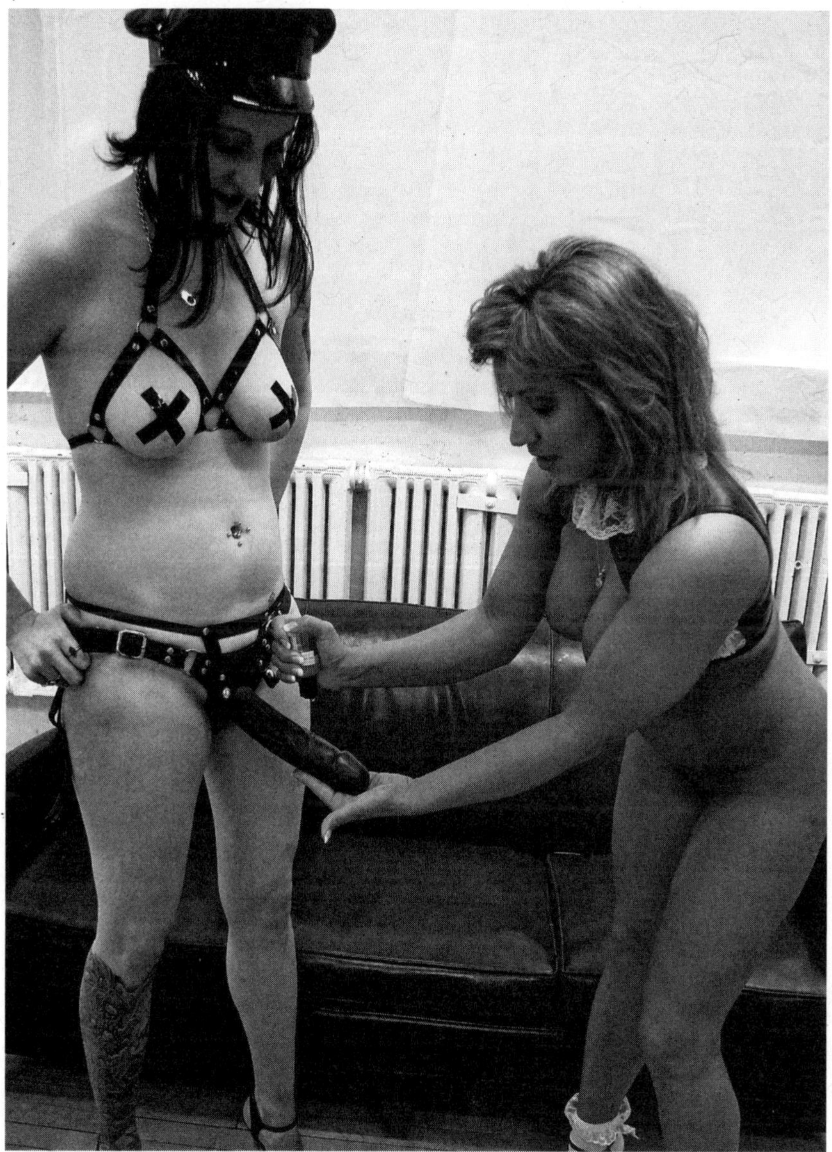

1 Lube lube lube! All slippery is the way to go!

Continues→

It just started out as an erotic set of photos for my Master, who had been out of town for weeks. I opened the fridge, grabbed a box of strawberries and headed to my room with my digital video camera. I got comfortable, undressed and spread my legs.

2 Bend over something, doggie style is best when first starting out.

3 Help guide them into you if they need it, since with a silicone cock they can't feel where your hole is like they could with a penis. Fuck away and get your lover to pull your hair!

I jumped a little from the coolness of the first strawberry as I rubbed it slowly on my clit, surprised at the sensation of the tiny seeds on my sensitive skin. I rubbed it gently along the soft folds of my labia, slipping the cool strawberry up and away inside me, tingling. I grabbed for a second, third, fourth, fifth...getting more and more worked up, until the entire box of strawberries was inside me. Then one by one, I reached inside myself and pulled out each little red berry, now hot, soft and covered in my juices. I moaned at the sweetness of the berries as I devoured them in front of the camera, making my fingers and lips sticky and pink. It was a lot more fun than I ever expected and a hot way to stay connected while we were apart. —doll, slave

Panic Snap: A type of snap sold in hardware or tack shops that can be released with a load applied to it, typically used with horses.

My favorite toy is my own vanity. I'm the first to admit I turn myself on. Call me vain, call me self-absorbed, but nothing gets me hot like my own reflection. I love watching myself as I get off. I am my best and first lover. I have been masturbating since the tender age of five, "blushing" as my mother called it. Throughout my years of experience I have been quite creative; pillows, armrests of chairs, the traditional washing machine, and the ol' pool jet. I even used Barbie doll legs, but that's another story. I'm older

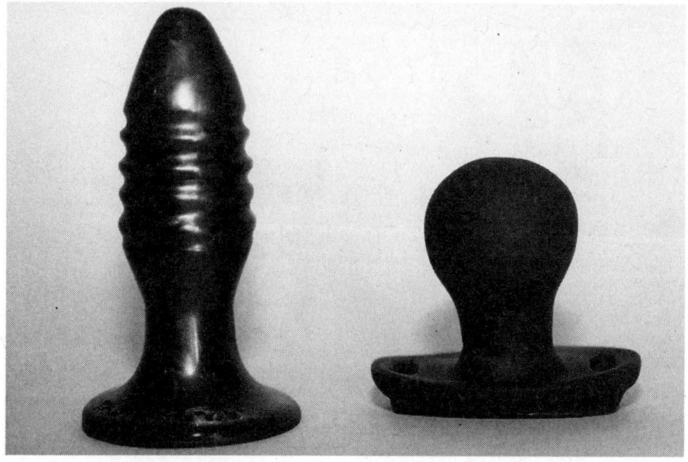

Two different types of silicone butt plugs. Each person's body is different; find what shape and size works best for you.

Pansexual: Relates to inclusivity of all sexes, gender identities and orientations for play or events.

now, and have quite a vast collection of toys, but nothing gets me off more than my vibrating dildo, complete with a suction cup, stuck to a mirror with me squatting over it so I can watch myself being penetrated. Some people like to watch another pussy get it while they pleasure themselves; I prefer watching mine.

—Ava Destruction, opportunistic hedonist

What's in My Heinie?

I have a game I like to play with newbies called Guess the Object where they are first stretched out comfortably and blindfolded, and then penetrated with a mystery object. The seductive qualities of having to guess what object is inside them can help focus their attention and increase their excitement level. Lots of improvised toys can be inserted and moved around, provided the object is smooth and rounded and the appropriate size. The handle of a butter knife is great, slender shampoo bottles, candles, mixing spoon handles—in fact, the kitchen is the place you will find the most easily pervertable objects. And that's where you'll find my favorite: vegetables, particularly the Japanese eggplant and zucchini that are soft-ish and don't break off inside someone like a carrot might. You can be sure that you aren't the first person in

Three different types of lube. Be careful which ones you use with toys; silicone toys should only have water-based lube used with them.

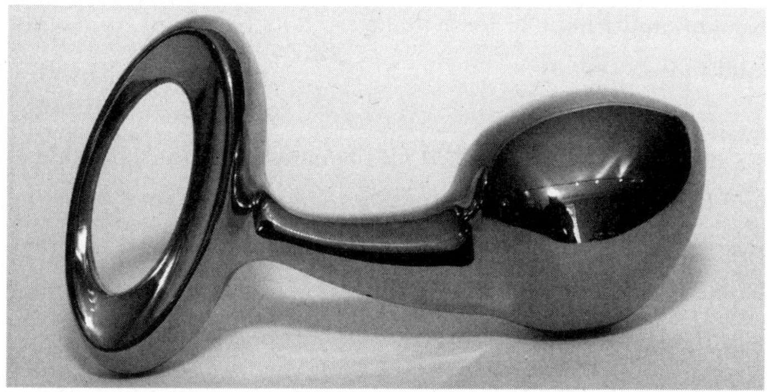

Stainless steel butt plug designed to stimulate the male prostate. Stainless steel can be put directly in the dishwasher or autoclave for cleaning.

the history of kinky sex to use these vegetables for more nefarious reasons than a nice salad! Wash them first, make sure there are no stems or other hard-edged bits poking out, and pull a condom over them before beginning. Using a condom is a great way for maintaining happy pussy pH balance in the vagina. Lots of lube is necessary to make sure everything is wet wet wet before beginning. If it is something going in the ass, hang on to it! The vagina is a dead end but the ass is not. If you lose something up a bum, refer to chapter 8, Safety. The best way to avoid a trip to the hospital to find out how far your ersatz sex toy went in the bum is to make sure it has a flared base or some other way to maintain your grip on it so it can't disappear inside your partner. No bottles or lightbulbs, please, if the glass isn't Pyrex (which some dildos are made of now); the chance for an accident to be catastrophic is more present than with other toys that are solid. If in doubt, ask your local sex shop for advice.

When penetrating the ass start with fingers and be gentle. You want to have your partner relaxed and receptive. Take as much time as you both want and don't be discouraged if he or she wants to try something else. What would be a better way to warm up a new bum?

"Okay honey, I have the whole evening to violate your ass. Did you get the lube? This plug is going in there at some point

Pervertable: Everyday, household objects like clothespins or candles that can be "converted or perverted" for kinky play.

tonight, and I hope it doesn't take too long because I have other stuff to do!"

Or:

"Hey sweetheart, I picked up the cutest little butt plug today and I thought we might play with it sometime tonight. Oh, by the way I also got some new massage oil and I thought maybe first I would treat you to a nice long sensual massage to relax you after your long day."

Which statement do you think is going to have them all warmed up and excited and eating out of your hand and ready for that cute little butt plug sometime later on that evening? People who are new to anal sex can be a little scared of it, so take your time and make it a warm and wonderful experience the first time. Massage their cock and balls or their clit; helping them achieve an orgasm the first time they have something in the "back door" will open them up to future possibilities. Above all else, don't rush it. If it isn't working or they are too tight, move on to something else for a little while and then revisit it. If you try to revisit it more than twice in one evening though, it will seem like you are getting pushy and you should save it for another evening. You have all the time in the world to explore with them, so take that time and make it a positive experience. For other anal toys like beads, again use lots of lube, take it slow and easy, and when they are getting close to an orgasm, pop the objects gently out in time with their orgasmic waves. This works best for men. Pull slowly—you aren't starting a lawnmower! One soft pop at a time does the trick.

My butt plug was such an eye-opening experience my first time: inserting it was like putting a 90-watt bulb in a 40-watt socket! One day my partner surprised me with a cute little blue butt plug. For a moment I was scared—despite its cuteness, it looked hard and thick—but I trusted him and wanted to try it out. Taking his time, he first relaxed me with an orgasm, then my new "friend" was introduced and he used lots of lube and was really gentle with my bum. After he slipped it past the first tight ring of muscle it settled in naturally like it belonged there. Going down on me again and eating my pussy, he then gently pushed two of his fingers into my pussy. I was receiving pleasure in three major erogenous zones and it was blowing my mind. When I reached orgasm, it was bigger than I ever felt before: a current oscillated though me endlessly, wave upon wave wracked my body. My little blue butt plug and I are now friends for life.

—Indiana, Stubborn Little Concubine

Percussion Play: Using an instrument designed to strike with force, typically a flogger, belt or cane.

A new term in the mainstream of sexual exploration is "pegging," which used to be called "strap-on sex." The old term may have intimidated some straight guys. Now that the act is being called "pegging" by marketing geniuses at sex toy companies it has become the new big trend. Straight boys are finally finding out what gay men have known for years: a prostate massage can feel great!

It was quite by accident that I discovered the lure of strap-on sex. My lover had picked up a leather body harness for me while away on a business trip. The top portion was straps that made triangles to showcase the breasts; the bottom straps wrapped around my hips with a ring in the center. One afternoon while I was playing with it by myself, I placed my dildo through the hole toward me while I masturbated. That was fun. Then I placed the dildo the other way, facing out. Wow! What an intense feeling of power. Then I remembered how turned on I had gotten when I read the scene in the book *Exit to Eden* where Mistress Lisa takes Elliott with a double dildo. Since then I've experienced great pleasure just walking around my apartment wearing the strap-on, feeling powerful and conquering. I feel the same thing when I fuck a guy up the ass while wearing the strap-on: watching the look in my lover's eyes as he experiences the pleasure of penetration, seeing a stronger climax as I own his ass.

—Mercury Kittie, Domme

Play Party: A BDSM event involving many people engaging in scenes.

Bondage: "Let's Get 'Em Tied Up!"

Bondage elicits feelings of helplessness, loss of control and being at someone's mercy. Helplessness is hot! Rape and gang bang fantasies when you are restrained are hot too! *Real* sexual assault: not so hot. Knowing that there is a big difference between the two will keep your fantasies and reality healthy.

You can do bondage without rope—the classic necktie or long silk scarf. Belts work too, as well as elastic athletic wrap. (Note: play should be fun but safety should be serious. One of the best books you can read on bondage safety before you get anyone tied up is Jay Wiseman's *Erotic Bondage Handbook*.) What else can you use to tie someone up with? Saran Wrap? I like to introduce newbies to bondage by using long women's scarves if they are shy or a little unsure about bondage in general. The restraint is there, yet they are extremely comfortable because the pressure is spread widely, and their excitement isn't tempered or cooled off by the scary looking three hundred feet of heavy hemp rope or chain spilling out of the closet. It isn't so important that you tie someone with super-expensive hemp rope imported from Japan; make the rope an indication of your intent, or your desire and will, rather than strictly fetishizing the rope itself.

Handcuffs are sexy. Really sexy. And someone will usually pick up a pair in travels through life and think, "Hey, I would like to try being handcuffed while having sex!" We all do. Really. However handcuffs are terrible for kinky playtime. They suck. Keep in mind their primary purpose—to restrain a captive in an authoritarian (*i.e.*, the police) manner. Handcuffs are made of hard metal, which is unforgiving. They bite in the wrong places and can damage the tender nerves and tendons in the wrists. They are designed to be uncomfortable—it keeps a suspect from moving around too much. They also have a tendency to be put on too tightly. And you will lose the key. That is pretty much a guarantee. Leave them at the store. No one ever had to unlock a scarf or man's necktie when playtime was over. I will show you how a simple four feet of a woman's scarf or piece of cotton rope will make

1 Don't make the initial knot so complex that it tightens down when he struggles. A simple knot tied twice should be enough to keep him secure.

2 Find the tightest part and work it free.

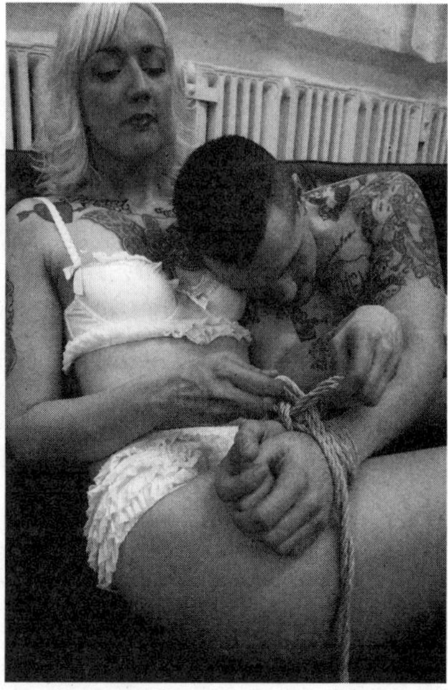

3 Once you get the knot loose, pull the tails back through the loops.

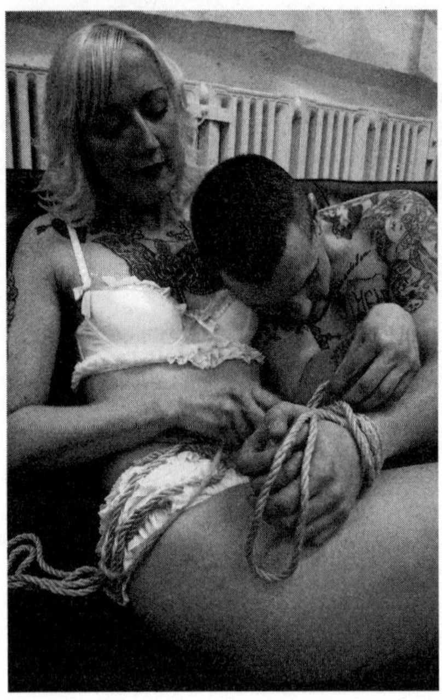

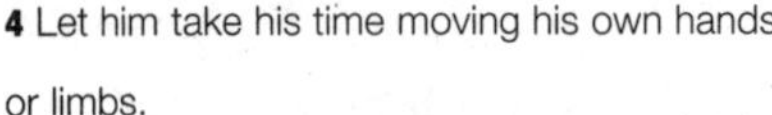

4 Let him take his time moving his own hands or limbs.

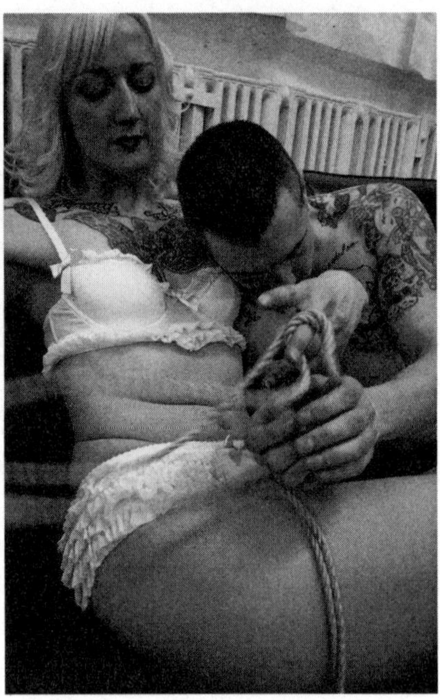

5 Reassure him that he has done really well.

for better and safer bondage in the bedroom!

For both scarves and rope you want to use easy-to-untie knots. It doesn't need to be complex at first. For those of you that fetishize knots and rope I highly recommend *Two Knotty Boys Showing You the Ropes* (see Resources), which will keep your fingers flying for a long time. Keep EMT scissors or a sharp knife handy and a pair of needle-nose pliers for knots that were put on with an extra bit of zeal.

Quick release is convenient if someone needs to get out quickly but it also allows for adjustment during "on-the-fly fucking" as people do squirm and ropes can get a little slack. You can just throw the quick-release end out of their reach but well within yours. Make the loop longer than their hand to keep it out of reach. When tying a submissive or slave to something the number one rule is make sure the object is stable! Lying down on an object such as a bed is a lot safer than standing on one foot. As a Top, you should always be asking yourself, What is the probable risk? You are going to juggle that extra ball in the air as well as many others flying in front of your face, such as scene atmosphere, role-play scenarios, impact, safewords, pinchy things, communication, and how to get your own desires and needs met as well. If you have someone tied to something and it falls over, immediately assess the situation and give first aid. You don't have first aid training? Why not? First aid certification is now being delivered especially for BDSMers. There are weekends where you get certified by the Red Cross for first aid and CPR, and all within a BDSM context. Organizers like me present these courses. After all, blunt force trauma is blunt force trauma, a sprain is a sprain regardless of whether you got it from a paddle or a rake handle that you stepped on à la some Warner Brothers cartoon.

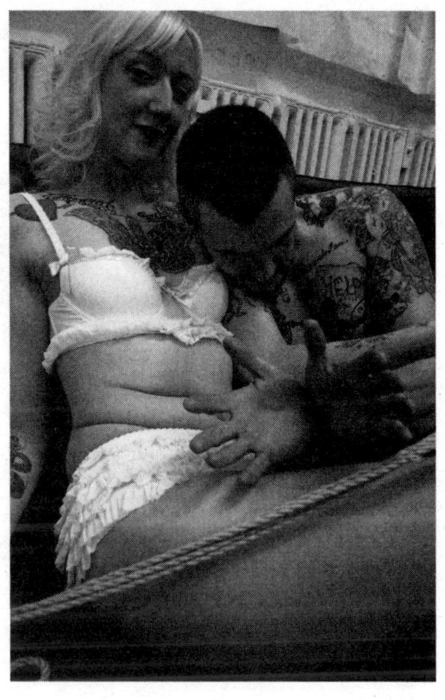

6 While they are cuddling in your lap, quietly straighten your rope and set it aside for later.

My favorite toy is definitely rope. It is as simple or complex as the skills of the person wielding it, and easily lends itself to instant inspiration. When I pack my toy bag, I include at least one set of fine quality bondage rope. I might have in my packaged bundle of six to eight 25–30' 6mm hemps for the base of my work, two to four 25–30' 8mm hemps for distributing weight loads or to add a heavier feel to a tie, and a couple 10' 4mm hemps for finer detailed work and/or hair and toe bondage. Added in are a swiveled suspension ring, carabiners, a pair of pliers, a rescue hook, rubber gloves, a couple of condoms in varying sizes, a bottle of olive oil, and a camera. With

A set of "Slave Steels"—collar, ankle and wrist cuff, requiring a lock to properly secure.

Pony Play: Sub is dressed in highly fetishized pony gear, complete with a mouth bit and anal plug with a tail. The Top or Dominant then makes her prance and treats her like a pony.

those basic toys in my crimson-lined leopard skin bag, I am ready for just about anything, whether my role is that of Top or bottom. Rope bondage can constrict, constrain and support the body while being capturing, nurturing, and repairing.

—Artemis Hunter, hetero-flexible Switch

Boys' and Girls' Genital Bondage

Genital bondage needs its own section since it is a little different from "regular" bondage—there's a higher risk factor involved. This isn't to scare you away from it, as it can be a lot of fun and very satisfying, but we use much smaller diameter rope or cord for this than you would for bondage to tie a person's limbs or body together and in using it on a much more delicate part of the body you need to use extra care and attention.

Cock and Ball Tying

For male genital bondage, start with a length of cord that is about 3' long. Parachute cord or cotton cord are great—you need something soft and pliable, that isn't going to be too distracting. What you are going to do with it will be distracting enough; you don't want the scene to end early because you used sisal cord on him and now his balls itch like mad and he can't concentrate on licking your stilettos! Household string is not thick enough—find something

Padded leather wrist restraints. Look for high-quality metal and leather parts when buying.

that's a minimum of 1/8" in diameter. Dental floss is NOT what we are going for—small and tough will bite into the skin and can even puncture it. It is important to remember that bondage for the bedroom is about getting your partner tied up as a starting point for other fun and games. Think of yourself as a spider that has to get that little fly comfortable in your web and eating out of your hand before you lay it on too heavy. Slow is easy, comfortable is easy. This is fun, so take your time. You can lotion up the balls with a nice hand cream to reduce chaffing, though it will make the rope a little slippery. Here are some basic steps:

Power Exchange: A defining characteristic of BDSM best described as "eroticism based on a consensual exchange of power."

1. Start with your 3' section and find the middle.
2. Cross the middle of the cord behind the balls, then bring the ends up to the top of the shaft and tie a nice overhand knot and snug it down. Then return to under the balls with the ends and make another overhand knot.
3. Wind between the shaft and the balls, nice and gently. Go slow; more wraps that are not tight are better than less-but-really-tight wraps. This will allow you to fine-tune the bondage. Don't go too tight: purple and blue are bad, unwind the cord if his balls are turning that color!
4. Finish the cord off with a nice bow behind the shaft or under the balls or some place unobtrusive that you can get to immediately.

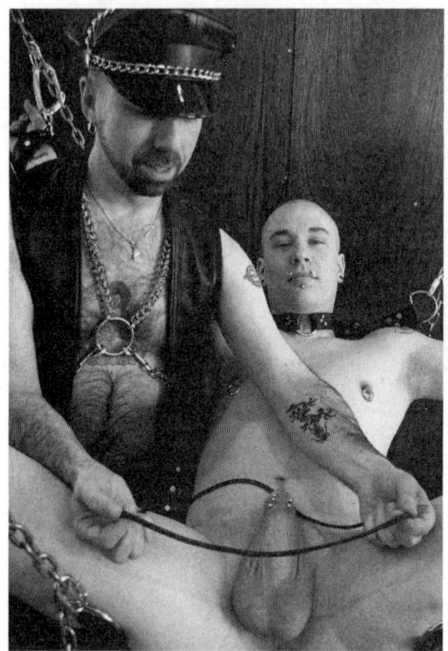

1 Take a nice soft piece of cord and find the middle.

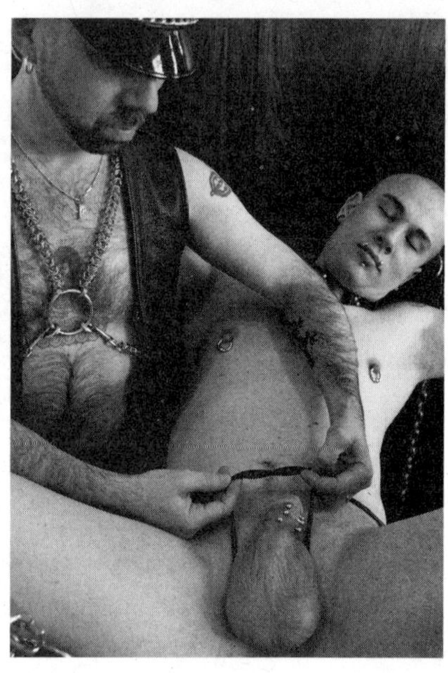

2 Loop it under the balls and up around to the base of the penis.

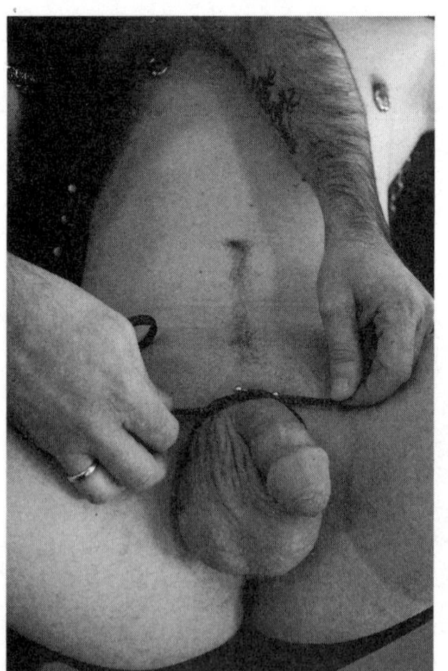

3 Make one overhand loop and tighten it snuggly but not too tight.

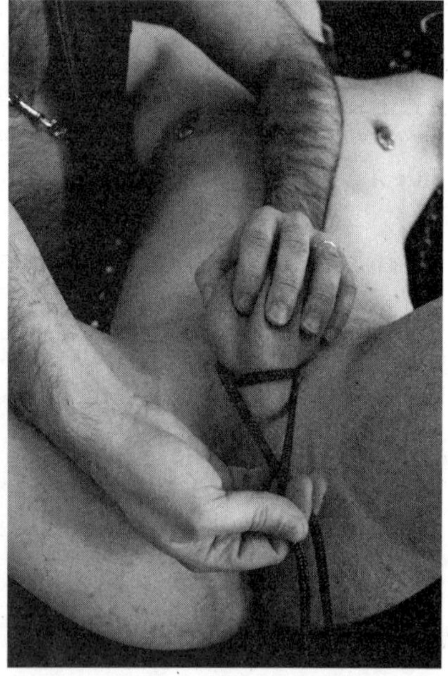

4 Then pull each end back down under his balls.

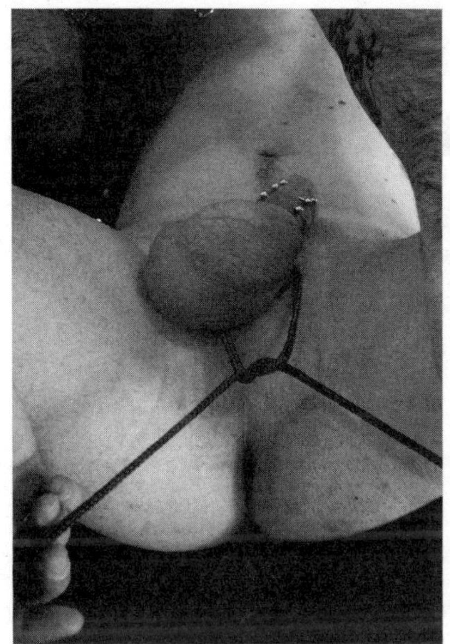

5 Tie another overhand loop and tighten it as well.

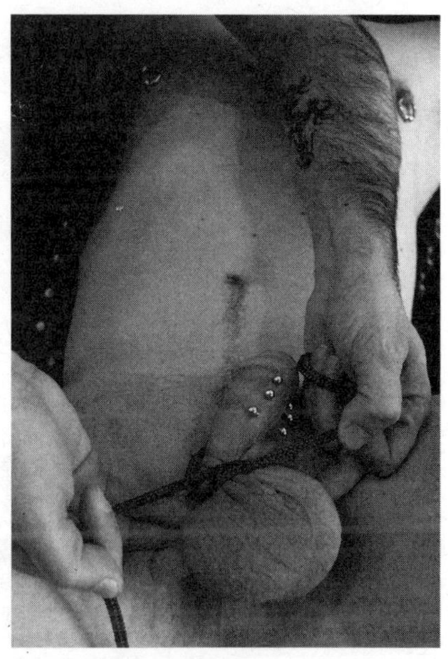

6 Now, start carefully winding the cord between the shaft of the cock and the balls.

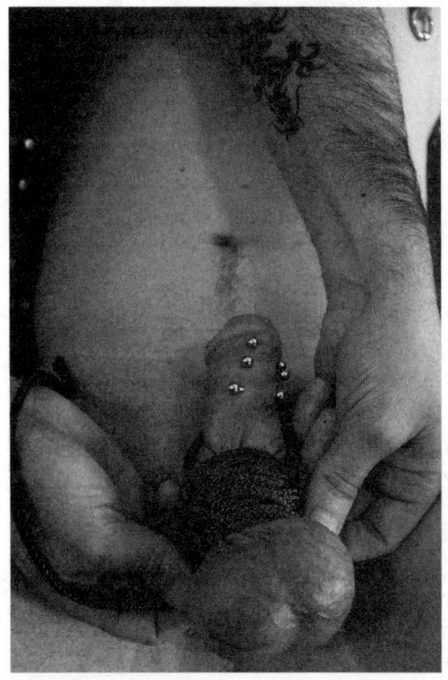

7 Keep winding (not too tight!) the cord, letting it pull his balls away from the base of his cock.

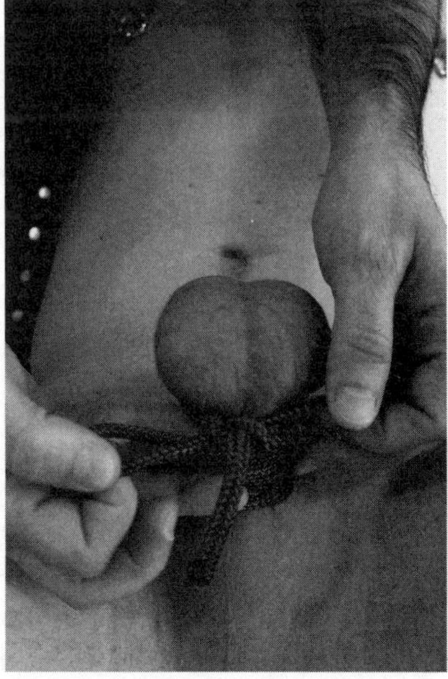

8 Finish it all with a bow that can easily be untied and enjoy!

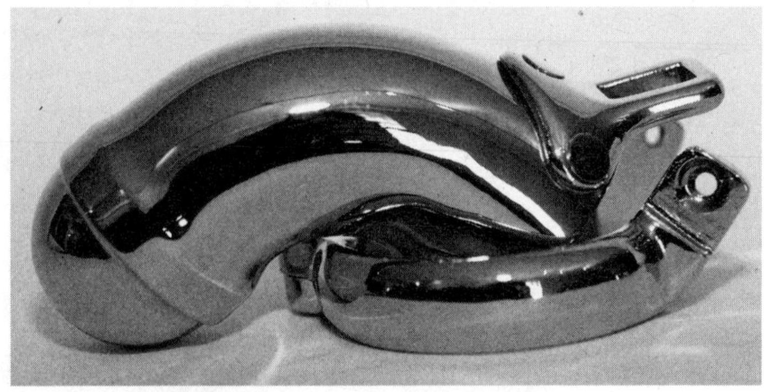

Lockable male chastity device, shown in the open (top) and closed (bottom) positions.

Pulling the balls away from their natural tendency to tuck up against the body will result in the ability to delay orgasm. Testicles are designed to tuck up against the body at the moment of orgasm, so this is a great way to make someone last longer and still stay hard. When you tie up a guy's genitals, especially around the shaft of the cock, the blood will be somewhat trapped in the cock and help it maintain an erection. Once it is like this, the tightness of the skin and the swollen member will make the skin more sensitive to fingernails, ice cubes, your mouth, feathers or anything else you can think of.

He CAN cum when tied up, but be forewarned that as soon as his orgasm happens you will need to take the cord off. What felt immensely pleasurable only minutes ago will start to feel excruciating or annoying after his orgasm. The cock and balls need to let fresh blood circulate through the body, so get it untied as quickly, but gently, as you can.

Protocol: Defined code of behavior that a partner is expected to abide by. Typically imposes limits on a submissive's behavior.

> I love when a boy is responsive and moans, groans, and swears reacting to the CBT that I'm inflicting. I like to have him tied to the coffee table faceup, where all the good parts are exposed. He gets very vocal in a whiny, crying way: "Please let me cum, my cock is so hard and red!" I tease him in a variety of ways, with just enough touch that his stiff dick knows I'm there, but not enough touching to satisfy the need, tormenting him. I know he wants to dump a huge load, but he doesn't have my permission to cum. —Benevolent Mistress of Chaos, Dominant

Female Genital Bondage

Women's genitals being the opposite of men's can be used to your advantage to tie a vibrator into her pussy, or a pair of balls or vibrating eggs. Spreading the lips with a nice hip harness is a great turn-on. Many women enjoy the position and sensations of being exposed, their legs splayed helplessly open, and you can heighten this sensation by also tying the outer pussy lips open to expose them or closed to secure something that is beyond her control inside her such as a remote-control vibrating egg.

Sensation Play

Sensation play has a much wider scope for toys; anything that can be trailed across the skin or teased or dripped along it can be used. Sensation play is where your creative thoughts can really work overtime! It doesn't have to be just skin-based sensations, it can also be aromatic or flavor based. There are multitudes of sensations you can create on and with someone; let's look at a few of the basics to get you started.

Riding Crop: A short, semi-flexible rod with a flat pliable end used in equestrian pursuits. When you first start to play, use only the floppy end to strike someone.

Hot Wax Candles

Find a low-temp candle. Dollar stores have great cheap low-temperature candles that usually have religious figures on them (yet another reason to use them during sex play). Don't use beeswax or high-quality paraffin wax. Hair is going to be a problem; it will usually come off along with the wax if you don't use a "release"—a greasy barrier that will help separate the wax from the skin. I recommend hand lotion for the area you will be dripping on. Shaving or depilation is an even better idea before doing wax play. Liquid candle wax is hot, so test it first! If you hold the candle up high above the person's body, the greater distance the wax has to drop through the air to the body will cool it marginally before it hits the skin. This is a great way to vary the temperature of the candle wax. Laying your partner down on his or her back and putting a blindfold on him is a nice way to make sure no errant drips of hot wax get in his eyes. Use old towels or bedsheets that can be designated as the "wax-play sheets," or you may want to use a plastic sheet. It is going to be messy and you have to accept that. Here is a cool bit of information for people interested in rope bondage: hemp rope loves wax! The wax will get all over the rope but when it gets worked into the fibers it will help moisturize them, so don't worry about cleaning them too much, just get the big chunks off and don't worry about the wax that has soaked into the rope. Cleaning methods for leather floggers are detailed on pages 104 and 105 of Jay Wiseman's book *SM 101* (see Resources).

I find that wax play is one of those really intense sensations that takes some time for a submissive to work through. Don't dump spoonfuls of wax on her, just take it drip by drip and let her skin and mind take the time they need to process it. Alternating ice cubes along with the hot wax is also a really interesting contrasting sensation that can go a long way to increasing the spectrum of your scene.

Floggers and Other Percussive Toys

Floggers and other percussive toys form the bulk of play instruments. Percussive instruments such as ping-pong paddles, rubber-

Two different floggers. The top one is made of deerskin with a braided handle and the bottom one is bull hide with a combination braided/metal handle.

Two horse hair floggers. The top has a fixed handle and the bottom has a longer, flexible handle.

handled spatulas, exquisite wooden paddles and of course leather and rubber floggers and single-tail whips are all going to fall under the same category but their methods of use and where they are used on the body for safe play vary. Some are perfect for the ass and legs and other instruments are excellent for the meaty upper back. Some do it all wonderfully and others are site specific. The first thing you will find when you are shopping for a flogger is that most look similar. They have a handle and all the tails are called a *fall*. The length, weight and choice of materials can make the similar looking floggers very different in how they feel when they strike.

Now that we know how the basic flogger is constructed, let's break down the four stages involved in flogging.

- ✔ potential energy
- ✔ kinetic energy
- ✔ follow-through
- ✔ alternating sensations

Role-Playing: Adopting roles such as "Hooker and John" or "Doctor and Patient" for a certain amount of time in order to explore aspects of those roles. Role-play can be either "fantasy" or "realistic."

The first is the setup of how to start with the flogging. This involves the stored or potential energy in the instrument. Note how the tails are held in line with the handle above shoulder height.

The second is the actual strike where all the potential energy is released into kinetic (traveling) energy. When flogging, the greatest kinetic force will be at the end of the tails. One flogger maker who is now retired made three beautiful floggers for me that had the tails cut so that they were a half inch wider at each end to deliver 50 percent impact.

The follow-through finishes the strike and returns the flogger to the setup position ready for the next strike.

Once you have mastered the art of the setup, the strike, and the follow-through, you can experiment with alternating sensations. Some simple patterns are the Figure 8, the Car Wash, the Towel Snap and the Drag. What you will notice quite quickly when you start breaking down the steps and get a rhythm is how naturally the flogger will want to return to the setup position if you have completed the follow-through correctly. You will start by holding the tails of the flogger out but in time you will feel the natural swing of the flogger and be able to judge where it "wants to be" in relation to the setup position for the next strike to be delivered.

For beginners, you should practice lightly at first. Even practicing on a pillow is good until you get the feel for the toy, the weight and the heft and how the fall of the flogger goes, the swing, and its weight. Alternate between hard and soft, stinging and slow; floggers can deliver a wide variety of sensations and it would

Anatomy of a Flogger

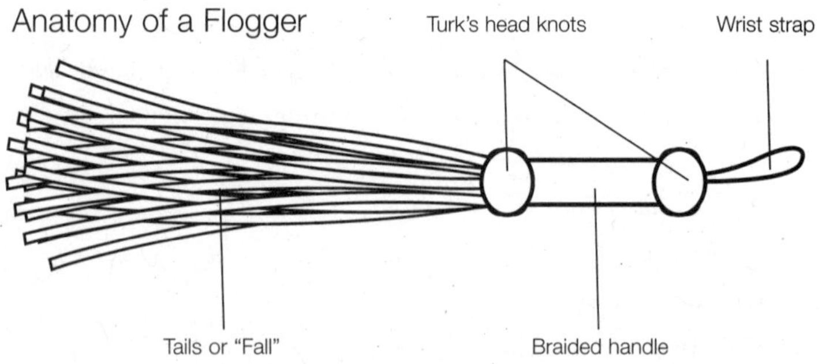

be a shame to waste your efforts on just one hard sensation. It is all about how you wield the flogger—it will become an extension of your desire and intent. You can even use the handle to poke and prod and in some cases, with a condom, insert it into a lucky submissive! Want a really heavy sensation? Take two different kinds of floggers made of different leather and cross their handles in your hand and then you can create heavy and stinging sensations at the same time! Since a person's body can get used to most sensations after about twenty minutes, you'll want to vary and mix it up to keep the sensations different. Hit the bum: it's fleshy and meaty and has a large muscle group. You'll do well to concentrate on the meaty parts of the body when flogging someone. Stay away from the kidneys and head!

Sadism: The act of administering pain for sensual/sexual pleasure.

Safety with Percussion

If a person tips his head forward you will feel a bump at the base of the neck; this is the C7 vertebrae and it is quite prominent in most people. Note that this spot and anything above it is off limits for anything but the softest sensations. The spine meets the head and carries with it nerves, veins, arteries, and a whole bunch of other delicate tissues that we don't want to damage. Irreparable damage can occur if any striking in this area is done with any force. You must be gentle and kind. If you want to protect this area during your initial work with your flogger, pull a T-shirt into a line and drape it across the nape of the neck. This offers a little bit of protection in case of an errant swing and it also gives you a visual reminder of where the off limits area is. A basic understanding of human anatomy will serve you well; go online or grab an anatomy book and study the basic musculature of the body. You should avoid directly striking the spine in general, but since it runs the length of the back it is difficult at first to do this. Rest assured that there is surrounding muscle on the top portion of the back to help cushion blows that land there. Aim for left or right of center of the back, where the big shoulder muscles are. Thick meaty areas of the body are where you want to strike,

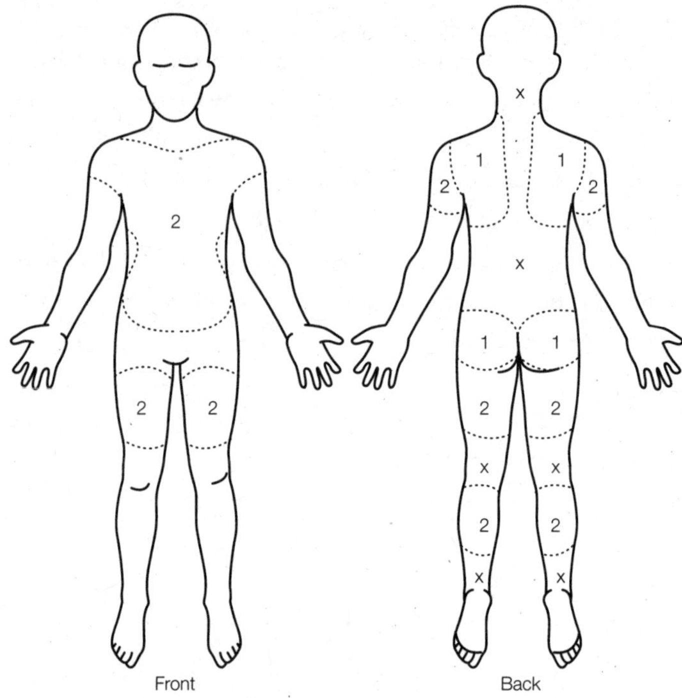

Where to flog on the body

1 Best (primary) areas for flogging.

2 Next best (secondary) areas.

X No hitting zones.

rather than places where the skin just covers the bone or there are joints. The ass, the back, the thighs and shoulders are all great places. Kidneys, lower back, joints, and tummy should be avoided. Breasts are another matter—while light flogging can be sensual and fun, medium to heavy blows may increase the risk for health issues later on. See chapter 8 for safety and breast-related concerns.

We always recommend for people just starting to experiment with power play to try something easy to use and not too expensive. You don't want to spend a lot of money on a toy and find out it wasn't really what you like after all. A soft short

> flogger or smallish slappers are good to start with because they are easy to use and offer a gentle thud sensation. Often people start with something softer to warm up; if you are inexperienced, at least you know you can't really hurt (in a bad way) with a soft flogger. It takes practice to hit well, in the right spot, and just the way your partner wants, so smaller and lighter implements allow you to make a few and not too serious mistakes along the way.
>
> —Sarah Forbes-Roberts, Come As You Are (a shop)

Safe Call: A previously arranged phone call at a specific time to a confidant after meeting or playing with a new partner.

Flogging is for fun and playtime, not for showing off how hard you can hit someone. Position of the body matters a great deal. The bottom should be standing upright, on his or her toes, legs taut, with the ass out and arms straight and placed against the wall. Being secured up on a cross is another classic position. However, having the sub lying down and stretched out on a spanking bench where he or she is about level with your waist is even better. That's my preferred position. It offers the Dominant or Mistress more opportunities for access to the body without him or her having to extend as much energy as the classic standing pose. And it offers a safer position as well; if the platform is stable there is much less chance of falling than when the sub is standing. When striking someone who is lying down, the flogger's tendency is to fall downward with gravity. Take advantage of this; you can deliver just as hard a blow this way with less energy than if you are striking out horizontally. You can walk 360 degrees around your victim and flog with a much wider variety of motion. Hold the tails so they gently brush the skin and sweep and stroke across the sub. Floggers come with just as many variations of tails as you can think of. Deerskin is lovely soft leather that sounds great but doesn't deliver too much impact while bull or moose hide are much heavier and will deliver more wallop.

Safeword: A code word that has been previously agreed upon to slow down or stop a scene. RED means stop, YELLOW —slow down.

No spanking bench in your home? Bending your lover across a table facedown conjures up its own images of role-playing fantasies; stretching her out on the bed does as well. Placing him

Sexual Exhibitionist: A person that becomes sexually excited by being the center of attention.

Sexual Voyeur: A person that becomes sexually excited watching others engage in sexual acts or play.

kneeling on the sofa, facing the back with his chest across the top, or up on his elbows is perfect for playtime. The cushions make kneeling a breeze and there's an added advantage if the sub is up on her elbows and hanging her head down between her shoulders. The shoulder muscles will flex and offer immediate protection for the before-mentioned C7 vertebrae and all the other delicate bits above it. Up on the elbows also gives you room to reach under and gently or cruelly stroke a dark engorged nipple that is hanging at the end of a juicy breast waiting in anticipation to be plucked like a ripe berry, or taut pecs framing dark areolae that beg for a sexy pair of clothespins to awaken their desires. Ass backward presents the Dominant with the genitals at a pleasing and convenient angle. I find this position superior to the classic standing pose. While I love seeing someone stretched out on a cross, waiting with bated breath for the next strike to fall, this position offers more variety and if performed on something stable like a sofa, the cushions will not only make the sub more comfortable but also offer a nice place to slide down into a prone position when the flogging is done.

Experiment with different positions; some will offer different parts of the body a better opportunity to be slapped. Let's not forget about the classic over-the-knee spanking. When you think of positions you want to try for flogging, keep in mind how it will facilitate your desires, coupled with safety. There will be a trade-off with every position. For example, if you bend someone into a ball you expose her kidneys but it also gives you better access to her strong shoulder muscles; if you strap him out tightly spread-eagle, you give yourself the opportunity to use toys gently on his cock and balls, but can't get at his buttocks for spanking. Take it easy and let common sense prevail; you want to hurt them and tease them, not damage them!

Once you both get the feel of each other, your play partner doesn't have to lie there like a bump on a log while you flog him. Have her move around and show through body language how much she loves what you are doing. Note, however, that there are bottoms

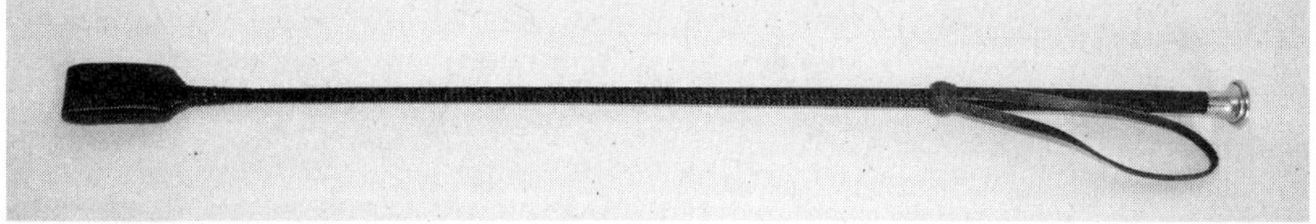

Riding crop. These are made in a variety of styles and lengths. For starting, pick one with a nice wide tip and a medium flexible shaft.

who get so deeply into being flogged and reaching subspace that they don't move around at all. This can be somewhat frustrating, and may seem as if you are only servicing their desires without getting any response in return. Personally, I like to have a submissive or bottom move and squirm and yelp and writhe—the struggling gets me off immensely. It gives me a very clear indication that what I am doing is really being taken and absorbed and "given back" to me. If you do have a partner who doesn't move around a lot, outside of a scene is the time to discuss your own needs, as in "I really would like to see you move around more and make it look like you are enjoying it—you just lying there isn't helping me into my own headspace as a Dominant." Never use "negative" or "blaming" language when you want to encourage someone. We aren't chastising at this point. This kind of bottom may well go so deep into subspace that he or she doesn't realize she is just lying there.

> As a bottom, the quirt [a short-handled stock whip with a forked tongue] has been my favorite implement of torture. It happens to be Sir's favorite toy, which certainly makes it more appealing to me, but there's more to it than that. The quirt demands attention. It can feel as if it is cutting into your flesh, much like a good cane. It can be merciless. That kind of pain takes me quickly into subspace, makes the endorphins rush, and pushes my will to submit—making me reevaluate and submit to Sir over and over with almost every lash. —Annie, Switch

A classic BDSM toy is the riding crop. It conjures up images of

Vise-style nipple clamps. This pair has threaded nuts that allow you to fine-tune how tight you want them.

prim and proper English riders with their jodhpurs, and smartly tailored jackets. This is a toy that can be used in a variety of ways to both stimulate good behavior and swiftly correct errant behavior.

I prefer the short-ended riding crop, which comes in varying lengths, thicknesses, and decorative touches, as it has always produced explosive responses in me. My first time experiencing this crop, it was being wielded by a cunning Switch who had a thing for manipulation and punishment scenarios. Blindfolded and kneeling, I was asked to lay out my hands palm-up while he produced an innumerable array of crops and whips, letting me feel their individual potential. Each one had its own special use and desired outcome; tassels that tickled or woven leather that stung. Once I had selected the instrument that appealed to me as being neither too hard nor too flimsy, I was ordered to strip bare and turn full circle under his gaze. I was told I'd been a naughty girl, and was forced to describe what wrongdoings I'd done to deserve such admonition. Experiences of being trapped in a confession booth during elementary school outings to the local parish flashed before my closed eyes. I'd always offered some kind of overexaggerated "sin" like swearing, or getting in a fight with my sister. But those things paled in comparison with what was happening that very moment. I found myself bent over his knees, asscheeks up, his hands fondling between them, my heart racing. My captor began to smartly brandish the instrument I had selected. Lying prone, I mumbled the number of strokes of whip on skin, and began to lose count after eighty-seven or so, my mind swimming and my ass in white-hot pain, which I loved. —Babyslut, submissive

Slave: A submissive involved in a committed Total Power Exchange (TPE) relationship.

Soft Limits: Something that someone is hesitant or nervous about doing but would like to try if they feel they are safe with you. For these people you need to go slow.

Percussion is a dynamic form of play in which adapting and improvising can be very sexy. In the kitchen with no flogger in reach? Try a wooden spoon or cheap plastic spatula. In the garage, but your whip is tucked neatly under some clothes in the closet in your bedroom? How about those paint stir-sticks sitting on the workbench?

My favorite toy is a man's belt. I love the quiet clink when the buckle is being undone and the soft hiss it makes sliding from around his waist and through the belt loops. It can be used for bondage and most of all for a wonderful whipping! I love the feel of it when it wraps around my body and its tail bites into my ass or thighs, and perhaps my nipples get a sharp flick when I am helpless before him and he uses it on me however he desires. Knowing that it is strapped around his waist at all times in public and that he might use it on me for correction of my behavior always makes me wet.

—Bliss, submissive

Don't forget that you always have a dependable pair of percussive toys with you wherever you go. When you want to go really old school, use your hands!

I have had everything from whisks to studded metal paddles to rabbit fur mittens used on me in a variety of strange and unusual ways, and by far the most thrilling "toy" I have at my

Submissive: The person that surrenders control either during a scene or all the time to another during erotic play.

disposal are my Master's hands. I have always loved the touch of my partner's hands, gentle or otherwise. There are some amazing sensations that only a specific manufactured toy can deliver, but in my opinion, nothing rivals the connection or intimacy of flesh touching flesh. It's a whole different level of commitment and it takes a certain kind of Dominant to do it. It's like the difference between people who garden with gloves and long-handled tools and those who go barehanded and dig with their fingers. I want the man with the dirt under his nails.

—Victoria, slave

Some other wonderful toys that will no doubt take up room in your toy bag are paddles and canes. Even though percussive *is* percussive, these instruments will create widely different sensations despite the essentially similar method of delivery: striking with force.

Almost anything can be a converted to a kinky toy with sufficient creative thought.

One day while wandering through a department store, I came upon this small neon-green tennis racket that described itself as an electric bug zapper. I took it home, put batteries in it and showed it to my roommate. You press a button to charge it and swing; one shot to the palm of our hands and I immediately put it away! A few days later I get home to find that my roommate had sold it to a Top friend of ours, thinking she was doing me a favor. I soon became well acquainted with Mr. Sparky, as it was named, and the Top used it to explore my ass at the next fetish event. At first the little click of the charge and the crack it makes when it connects was a deterrent, but now it is one of my favorite sounds in the world

—Tracy, submissive

My favorite toy? It's an electro dog collar that Master has retrofitted to fit around the balls. The remote control is designed so

A padded blindfold is more comfortable and blocks out the light better.

that it delivers a single jolt and can't give a continuous charge. There are eight different levels. I've managed to get to level five with just flinching. Levels six to eight still get growls, moans, or screams depending on where my head's at. Nothing like getting that quick jolt in the balls from across a crowded bar to let me know that Master wants me!

—Master C's slave Dan

Playtime doesn't have to be so hard core that you wind up being strapped down to a table in an evil mad scientist's lair (although that does sound like a pretty tasty start to a role-play) filled with all kinds of buzzy and zappy things. You can just get started with something as simple as a vibrator. Imagine how kinky it was when it was first developed for the medical practice one hundred years ago to treat women's "hysteria." That's a prescription most would enjoy.

My fortuitous discovery of the Hitachi Magic Wand changed my life. This two-speed massager is advertised as a muscle relaxer; place it vibrating against a clitoris and you can immediately understand the massive female worship of this exceptional instrument. Upon my first encounter with the Magic Wand I reached a climax the likes of which I was previously

> unaware my body could attain, and squirted all over the floor! Since then it has become a staple item in my continuous expedition to find the apogee of pleasure. —Sabrina, submissive

Getting Someone New Comfortable with Toys

Picture this: you have met an exquisite newbie who is interested in exploring with you but is intimidated by floggers, whips and chains. How do you convince her that her life really would be much more complete if she let you fix your new clover-leaf nipple clamps to her areolae? Or some other such toy? This can be a scary and exciting time for someone who is new to kinky sex and the bottom line is that, regardless of whether they are bratty or shy, if they are truly interested they want to be reassured that it is going to be fun and not harsh. What I like to do with a new toy or new partners is demonstrate it to them, show how I would use the toy and show my skill level. I let them pick out a toy they are curious about and then I use it on myself or them, so they can see the reaction it causes. After all, nipple clamps aren't really as intimidating as they initially look.

Things to Remember About Toys

- ✔ You don't have to spend a lot of money on toys to have fun.
- ✔ Your toys are only an extension of the creativity in your own mind.
- ✔ Support local sex toy artisans when possible.
- ✔ Learn to demonstrate a toy on yourself.
- ✔ Listen to your partner's feedback, and use it to your advantage.

> I saw at a kinky craft fair a pair of nipple clamps with a beaded chain that can be worn as a necklace; my submissive now wears them under his shirt when we are out in public. I've put weights on his nipples, hot-waxed them, and licked and teased them while the clamps sharply bite into them. The best part is that moment where my submissive looks in my eyes as I am about to take the clamps off and the blood rushes back in, because it hurts the most but only for a quick second. I love having the power to give him pain or pleasure and once he's in that situation with the clamps on, there's only one way out and that is to make me happy.
>
> —Electric Melissa, ass-kicking gal

Bottoms and submissives want to know that you are not only competent but also that you can wield that toy in a masterful way. Can you take those anal beads that you are waggling at them up your own butt comfortably? It is very reassuring to newbies that you HAVE put the time and energy into your own education and skill set to learn the subtle nuances of the toys you own. Did you put in the hours and hours to learn the single-tail whip on your own? Have you spent time flogging pillows and then graduated to people, and know how to use it to its full advantage? If you make your skill-set development of paramount importance to play, if you haven't just picked up a nasty looking quirt from your last trip to Mexico the day before and are looking for a bottom to welt with it, that will make you much more attractive to any potential play partner. If it is your first time out with a new toy, be honest! Be up front and say, "I just picked up this delicious handmade flogger last night, do you mind letting me try it out on you if I go gently at first? You get to pop its toy cherry!" This sounds a whole lot more seductive than "Hey, I just got this stick-looking thing and have never tried it before, let me see what it can do to your ass!" As a bottom or submissive, if the Top is wielding something harsh looking and it is out of your comfort level, don't be shy about letting him or her know. It's your ass on the line. Being open with your communication will make you desirable as a play partner, not retreating into silence when you are asked a question like "What kinds of bruising is this going to cause and how do I treat it, since I am going to the gym tomorrow?"

Chapter 8

Safety

What do you do if the person you are playing with has diabetes and her blood sugar level drops? What is your partner supposed to do if you have epileptic or an asthma attack? Perhaps you have a trick knee from an old sports injury that has a tendency to pop out of its joint when it gets twisted the wrong way? Dom and sub are **both** responsible for a safe play environment and for addressing health issues that may arise. These issues should never come as a surprise. Have you both communicated any pertinent personal health information so you know how to respond appropriately? Responsibility for safety falls squarely on you and your partner. If you hurt someone because of thoughtlessness or ignorance then you are ultimately liable for it and that is a heavy responsibility to bear. Play should be fun but safety should be serious.

There has been an exhaustive amount of research done on safety within BDSM. Safety education is a long process, and having your certification in first aid is a good place to start. I can't spell out all of the issues that can go wrong during playtime and

Sub Drop: A physical condition sometimes experienced by a submissive after an intense session of BDSM play, best prevented by providing aftercare immediately following the session.

how to fix or address them. This is why I highly recommend two seminal books on the subject: *On the Safe Edge* by Trevor Jacques and *SM 101* by Jay Wiseman, for starters as well as others. This chapter will address some of the key issues in safety as a rough guide only; you should always seek the aid or advice of a medical professional for any serious health issue.

Emotional and Psychological Safety

Consent, consent, consent. We don't indulge in kinky play without the consent of another. There can be no coercion or begging involved; it must be a consensual exchange of sexual and physical energy. One of the most delicious feelings we can experience in kinky sex is the feeling of surrender, of opening up physically, emotionally and mentally. With this feeling of exposure comes the responsibility of making sure your partner is experiencing it in a positive way. We can reassure our partners in many ways. Physically we can offer reassurance during playtime and cooldown; never underestimate the power of cuddling and holding either before, during or after a scene. Using positive "I" language is important when you are communicating with them; never use blaming language. If you ever need to correct their behavior, you might want to use that Oreo method we talked about in chapter 4. This is where you frame what you want corrected between two positively reinforced behaviors or actions in order to positively reinforce the ideas, behaviors, duties or concepts you want them to accomplish or embrace, for example: "I really love it when you are kneeling on the floor with your cheek pressed to the cold ground and your ass is nice and high, but if you arch your back a little more for me the way I like it, it will look extra slutty and it'll feel much better when I am spanking you." This delivers clear feedback so they know what they do well and what they can do better, all with positive language.

A tone of respect is important. In an established relationship between a Dominant and submissive, the Dominant needs to

Bound, spread open and helpless is a great way to spend a Saturday night!

Subspace: A "natural high" or endorphin rush that a sub can get during a scene.

be able to pick up on body language and other visual cues, especially if the sub cannot verbalize that something is wrong. Ideally, they should pick up on it right away, for instance, through a predetermined action (*i.e.*, the submissive's safeword is replaced by an action such as dropping a small object). If

Switch: Someone who likes being both Dominant and submissive, either in one scene or on different occasions.

these cues are not attended to, and a "rupture" in the fabric of trust is exposed, it is invariably worse to say nothing or do nothing out of fear of looking inexperienced. Open the door to communication immediately without being disrespectful. A simple "Please tell me what is going on, baby," can be sufficient. It is also the submissives' responsibility to communicate their concerns—dialog and communication go two ways. If something goes wrong, whether it be the result of a physical or emotional trigger, a responsible and caring partner will contain the situation. When people are in a vulnerable place, they may feel as though their entire being is going to disintegrate or destruct—that if they don't have a strong person there to guide them, they could shatter. They need to feel as though they are figuratively being held and be confident in the knowledge that the moment is contained and they are safe.

—Allison Hughes, clinical social worker

Does "no" mean "no" in playtime? Of course it doesn't. These are often uttered in the course of kinky role-playing in the bedroom and dungeon and that's why safewords have come to be used to slow down or stop a scene. (See earlier discussion in chapter 3.) Green, Yellow and Red have developed into a universally accepted triad of terms unique enough to not be said mistakenly and immediately identifiable. If you are playing with gags then an accepted alternative is to place a set of keys in the bottom's hand and have him or her drop them as "Yellow," which then gives you the opportunity to remove the gag and ask her to tell you what is wrong or needs adjusting.

Bondage Safety

Anytime anyone gets tied up there has to be a quick way of getting that person free should an emergency develop. If the tie is done with rope or leather, EMT safety shears are a must to have nearby. For rubber or plastic wrap, you may want to use seat belt cutters. I don't as a rule carry a sharp-bladed knife (unless I am

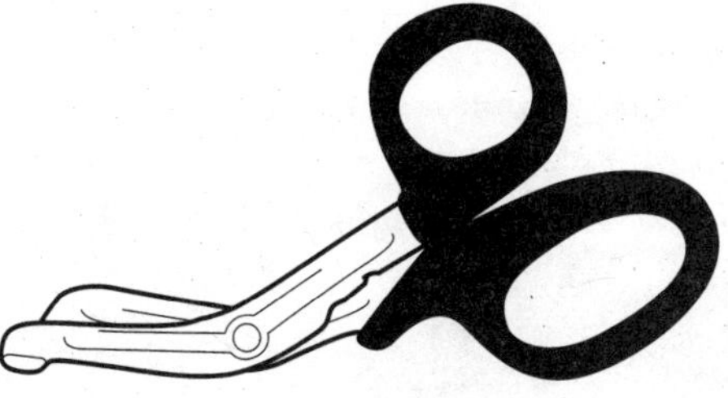

Snub-nosed EMT shears for safe emergency rope-cutting.

Training: Refers to either a short or ongoing period of time in which the Dom/me teaches the sub how to act in a specific situation. Can either be playful or serious, depending on the couple.

doing a knife-play scene) as a safety precaution; I much prefer snub-nosed EMT shears. The advantage to them is if your fingers are all lubed up and things are slippery the chance of damaging someone while trying to free him or her with EMT shears is much lower than if you are holding on to a razor-sharp knife with lubed-up slippery fingers. You don't want to increase the danger or the issues by cutting them inadvertently when all they need is to be free. There are many ways of using rope that can expedite the process of getting them untied. What I have found with rope bondage is that it tends to go a little more slowly than other methods of bondage—but because of that you can fine-tune the bondage, loosening or tightening areas, and seldom have a problem spring up on you. The bottom can feel his fingers falling asleep long before they actually do and communicate that to you so you can adjust the rope accordingly. If you are going to put rope on a person, you need to make sure you don't tie knots on top of knots. This is a mistake that many make in the haste of passion. As the Dominant you need to be able to get at those knots and untie the person quickly if need be. (See slip knots photos on pages 96–100.) Buckling someone into wrist restraints has the bonus of your only needing to unbuckle a strap to free her. Tying someone's hands above his head for long periods of time will cause the hands to fall asleep, and if they are stretched upward, this may cause difficulty with breathing if the torso is pulled taut, as the diaphragm will not be able to function correctly.

Ball gag. This type has a silicone ball which is softer and easier on the teeth, and a leather strap.

Trigger: An emotional/mental or physical activity that causes a distinct reaction. Comes in both the Good and Bad kind. Be sensitive to your partner's trigger(s).

There are a multitude of things that CAN go wrong with bondage; I want you to have a safe and fun playtime, whether in the bedroom, the kitchen, the den, a sleazy motel room or a fetish party play space. A nice simple spread-eagle tie on the bed is a great and safe way to start. Don't be so overwhelmed by safety issues you're afraid to play, just make sure you are playing within your comfort zone and that you know you can handle issues immediately and effectively. When you have your partner bound, staying in contact with her, emotionally and physically, is essential. You aren't just "playing" around—you are responsible for that person's safety. Fire, earthquakes and the like are all long shots but Mother Nature has been known to work in strange ways. Be prepared to respond quickly to unexpected emergencies. Above all, never ever leave someone in bondage alone. EVER. Do not go to the store or out for a beer and leave them behind chained up in a box. Any partner who requests that you leave him or her or wants to leave you alone, bound, should be avoided no matter what "fail-safe" methods he assures you are in place. The number one cause of death in bondage accidents is the victim being left alone, either by choice or left there by someone. People who engage in private, self bondage always increase the risk to their safety. Sometimes they do it because they have no one else to play with, or perhaps they have a spouse that doesn't understand their desires or simply no one who's interested in the same activity. Some enjoy the perceived thrill of being helpless and left only to their own wits to "escape." I highly recommend that anyone who wants to play with bondage does it with a partner.

Trust: The most important aspect in all of BDSM.

Gags

Gagging someone can be a very powerful experience, both mentally and physically. Rubber ball gags look very sexy in bondage pinup pictures but will cause a person to drool an amazing amount, so be prepared for it to be messy ten minutes after you get the ball buckled in. Some people like ring gags which is a metal ring instead of a silicone ball—I have a preference for ring gags as they give the submissive or bottom the feeling of being helplessly gagged but it does not obstruct their airway. Stuffing panties or stockings into the mouth can be a lot of fun but don't tie them there as there is a chance they can slip down into the back of the throat and cause choking. The submissive should be able to spit them out in the event of an emergency.

Drinking and Playing

Stay off the sauce when you are playing. Alcohol is okay in moderation but it is very difficult to reassure that new bottom you want to play with at the latest fetish night that you are very good with the cane after you have had six to eight martinis. Drugs should be avoided, as they alter your perception of reality, not a good idea for someone wielding a whip. Getting all liquored up, buying a new whip and then demanding someone play with you is just a recipe for a disastrous weekend.

Sexual Health History

Know who you are playing with. Take time to discuss and communicate emotional and physical health issues, then base your level of play on that communication. What about their blood health issues? Have they been exposed to one of the hepatitis viruses or are they HIV positive? What can you do to protect yourself while still enjoying playtime with them? Choices about partners are just as important as any other negotiations. Never let your ego get in the way of

Total Power Exchange: A relationship based on D/s where the Dom/me has ultimate authority over the submissive.

your sexual health. Choices you make could affect you for the rest of your life. Do you know how to use latex condoms effectively not only on toys and penises but also perhaps slitting one down its length and using it as a dental dam if you don't have one available?

> Sadomasochists have made ourselves extremely knowledgeable on the subject of AIDS and health—[People should] periodically take the AIDS antibody test. Almost all of us, even those with negative test results, have restricted or limited our own play and/or choice of partners in some way. Indeed, we now are seeing a new challenge in our play: to eroticize the use of condoms and gloves and other necessary safety measures in a creative manner.
>
> —Charles Moster and JJ Madeson, *Bound to Be Free*

Toy Safety

If you keep one toy for a specific person, that helps ensure there is no cross contamination although that toy still needs to be cleaned. Unfortunately that isn't always practical for most budgets. So to prevent any cross contamination you need to thoroughly clean and maintain your toys, especially insertable ones such as dildos, ass and pussy toys and also gags. Anything that will come into contact with someone's body fluids will need to be cleaned much more thoroughly than something that does not.

> Many bacteria and viruses are susceptible to drying. HIV is a fairly fragile virus if it is not in a bodily fluid but others can live on, say, a butt plug for months, even if it stays dry. So no matter how long your toys have been laying around since they were last played with, they should be decontaminated before being used again.
>
> —Trevor Jacques, *On the Safe Edge: A Manual for SM Play*

Jacques also recommends the following cleaning solutions: chlorine bleach diluted in water at a 1:9 ratio, or 70 percent isopropyl

1 Face sitting is a really fun and sexy adventure for both of you! Sexy torment works best while you are wearing panties—it makes the woman less accessible and thus more desired. Continues→

2 Have your bottom lay face up on the floor, bed, or couch. Lift your sexy legs over him to straddle his face, either facing away from or toward his head. This puts you in a superior position above him and gives you control over what happens and when.

3 Make him beg for the chance to have you sit on his face. Make him say all the nice things you like to hear and tease him before lowering your crotch onto his face, and taunt him with restrictions such as, "No licking but you may kiss through my panties."

alcohol to water mix (which comes premixed at the drugstore), and also Betadine, a brand of consumer available povidone-iodine topical antiseptic. One can also mix a half and half solution of Betadine and isopropyl alcohol in a spray bottle. Toys need to be washed after playtime and then again just before they are used—bedside nightstand drawers aren't the most sterile of places after all; do you really want to put that dildo in with a dust bunny attached to it? Just using soapy water to clean a toy isn't enough to ensure its safety. It's a great start but is not the only step. A preventative step before using a toy is to cover it with a condom. This is easy and quite quick for toys you are going to share. Used properly, this introduces another physical barrier and is easily disposed of after play. When removing the condom from the toy, ensure that you do so in a manner that easily and cleanly takes the condom off without

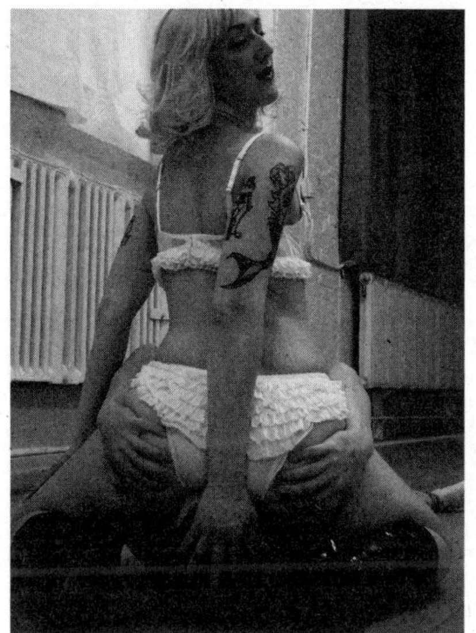

4 Push your beautiful ass down onto his face and cover his entire face. Once he gets into it and gets excited his breathing will increase. The secret to a good face-sitting session is to torment him until he starts to have to fight for air. Then lift up off him and let him get a breath.

5 Vary the sensations—there is the Long Crush which makes them fight for air. There is the Bucking Cowgirl where you repeatedly lift up and then smoosh your crotch back into his face, the Grinding Girl where you dry hump his face.

any contamination: securely grip the base of the condom and then stretch and lift it back up the shaft of the dildo so you don't touch any part of it and the condom winds up inside out when it is off the dildo. You still have to use your best judgment and common sense when cleaning and maintaining your toys, but these methods can give you yet another level of reassurance.

There is a big difference between cleaning toys and sterilizing them. Sterilizing occurs when the object is placed in an environment above 300 degrees F for over a half an hour (such as an autoclave, which is a strongly pressurized device designed to heat water above its boiling point to achieve sterilization). Most toys are okay to use if they are simply cleaned but if you are using something that will puncture the skin you need to take the next step up and sterilize it.

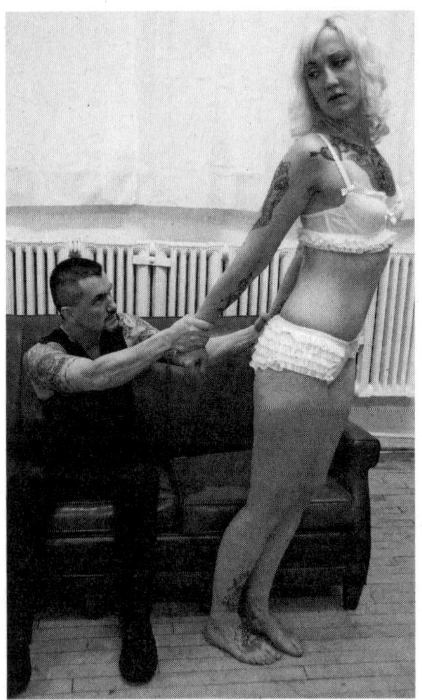

1 Take your partner firmly.

2 Pull her across your lap.

3 Fold her wrists behind her back and hold them there.

4 Pull her panties down firmly, tell her she has been a bad girl and needs to be spanked.

5 Make a firm, open palm, keeping your fingers together.

6 Hit the fleshy part of her bottom, alternating between hard whacks and smooth touching. Tell her it is for her own good.

Top Drop: Similar to "Sub Drop" but can affect a Dominant or Top after a scene. Feelings of guilt are commonly associated with it and aftercare helps counteract this.

While most plastic, jelly or hard-shelled dildos can be placed in the dishwasher, some are sensitive to heat. Cyberskin—a soft squishy polymer-based toy that emulates the feel of human skin, (also known as SoftTouch and Euroskin) is going to warp and melt terribly if you put it in the dishwasher. I much prefer silicone-based toys, which can be boiled or cleaned with mild soap and water. Silicone-based lube should NOT be used with silicone toys as it can damage them, and if you nick or cut them, a small rip will quickly turn into a larger one, so be careful about having it in your mouth or around other sharp objects, or being overly anxious in fitting it in that new strap-on harness you just bought.

Floggers and Whips

What about floggers and whips made of leather? The first rule is, don't break the skin. You can avoid a lot of blood health contamination issues if you don't go so hard that you cause the submissive to bleed. Know who you are playing with! If your partner has blood- or fluid-related issues then you have to assess those risks for your own health. A cracker, the nylon string at the end of the whip that makes the scary sound, should be considered a one person only toy or disposable. Be forewarned when using your new leather flogger on someone, if you get cum and lube or other fluids on it, you are not going to be able to clean it effectively. There are leather cleaners and conditioners to remove dirt and keep the leather supple but you will not be able to guarantee that the flogger is clean for the next person if you allow it to become soiled by fluids. That's an important consideration if you have just spent three hundred dollars on a brand-new bull-hide flogger. Personally I prefer to be proactive; I simply don't let fluids come in contact with my leather floggers. If someone's pussy is slick and wet then I don't strike her there. I don't hit anyone hard enough to cause the skin on the back to break and bleed. However if you WANT to have your pussy or cock and balls slapped around, buy a toy specifically for yourself, preferably one made of plastic, rubber, or PVC that can be washed and cleaned effectively.

Oh No, Where Did It Go?

Bum safety: first of all, you will most likely be stuffing something up there sooner or later, be it a finger or a dildo or a plug, or a vegetable. Your curiosity will get the best of you, and ass play can be a lot of fun. Take some time to learn about your bum, most of the nerve endings are concentrated right near the beginning at the anus so it responds best to stimulation and pressure. Men have the prostate gland (also known as the male G-spot) which can feel intense and really good when stimulated either externally or internally, and a woman can have the internal body of her clitoris stimulated. When most of us think about the clitoris we only take note of the little bit poking its head above the surface at the top of the vagina, when in fact it is a much larger organ that wraps around the vagina and urethra. Extending down and back from the clitoris head is a mass of erectile tissue called the "bulbs" filled with nerve endings which swell with blood and extend back inside the body, connecting to other organs including the rectum and anus. With anal insertion, take your time and learn what feels good and what doesn't. This isn't a race, slow down if you are feeling vulnerable or overwhelmed. Breath and relax, and if it still hurts then don't do it. Choose your object carefully, nothing with sharp edges should go anywhere near the anus, including fingernails, which should be short, rounded and smooth. Lube, lube, lube it all up! The more lube the better since, unlike the vagina, the anus doesn't make its own lubricant.

Things to Remember about Safety

- ✔ Consent is paramount. We don't coerce someone into play.
- ✔ Never leave anyone alone in bondage EVER.
- ✔ No drinking or drugs while playing.
- ✔ Make sure any toy to be inserted is smooth and rounded.
- ✔ Know who you are playing with and their sexual health.

There is a chance you might lose one of your toys up there, which is why whatever you use should have a wider flared base or handle on the end to hold on to. This will perform two functions; it won't be able to accidentally slip up into someone and it will give you something to hold on to when removing it. The vagina is a dead end but the rectum isn't and there is a deeper place for lost objects to go.

Sharing erotic experiences together will bring you closer together. Keep an open mind and have fun.

If you lose something in the ass that will not cause damage by scraping the inner lining of the rectum, such as ass balls or a dildo without a pair of "balls," remember that the ass is designed to eliminate solid or semi solid objects. In a panic, perhaps caused by losing an object in the ass, the human nervous system tends to shut down peripheral functions, such as bowel movement, causing the sphincter muscles to tighten. To help alleviate this problem, try to reassure the person containing the lost object, thereby switching those functions back on. What goes up normally comes down. However if something breaks while in the ass, we recommend that you leave the task to the Emergency Dept of your local hospital.

—Trevor Jacques, *On the Safe Edge: A Manual for SM Play*

Clamps

Oh fun! Clothespins or metal nipple clamps, even chopsticks wrapped with rubber bands on the ends can make whatever's sticking out VERY sensitive. A clamp pinches the skin and pushes the blood away from it. When the clamp is removed the blood rushes back in and causes an intense sensation. The longer it is left on the more intense that sensation is going to be. However you should never leave the clamps on long enough for the nipple or skin to turn purple. Purple = bad. Conversely snakebite kits or a bell kit are the opposite of a clamp—they cause blood to be pulled in forcefully to the skin and engorge the nipples or clitoris or whatever else you have trapped in there. The skin will become even more sensitive to touch. Again, the color purple is a bad sign—alleviate the clamp or suction device before it gets to that point.

Kinky sex increases the chances for heightened awareness and heightened risk in your sex life. As we have seen there are many issues to keep in mind when playing. Some people like to engage in much more extreme forms of kinky sex and for them I suggest they find an expert who is actively engaged in those activities who is willing to teach them. Play hard but play safe. Use your common sense and good judgment, for you are ultimately responsible for your own health and safety and that of your partners.

Chapter 9

Calling In the Professionals

A long slender leg sheathed in a leather boot, her riding crop tip playfully toying along the arch of her foot, hair in a severe bun and eyes broadcasting a dominant strength that makes you feel your place is to kneel before this Woman, this Dominatrix, this Goddess... You've seen those photos, the ones that make your submissive heart jump into your throat and create a stirring deep inside you. What if you don't have the time or resources to find a partner that you can develop a long-lasting kinky relationship with? Enter the professional Dominatrix or "Domina." While there are professional male Dominants, the majority of the industry is female led; that is the reality of the industry. There are many reasons why someone chooses to take his desires to a professional. He may feel that the anonymity of the situation can free him from the social restraints of his vanilla life and let his sexuality soar, albeit for just a little while. Some people prefer the convenience of worshipping a Domina for an hour or two as a nice diversion from their mundane office jobs—something to

Uniform Play: Incorporates role-play with the wearing of uniforms. Many people find the wearing of uniforms and their inherent symbolism arousing.

put a little spark back in their day, to send them back to the office after lunch feeling their newly welted ass sore and tingly, reminding them of the fun they had, while stuck in a budget meeting for the rest of the afternoon. The reasons why individuals might want to retain the services of a professional are as diverse as they are themselves.

If you want to go see a pro, there are some rules of etiquette you need to know: how to conduct yourself, and what to expect from the professional. How do you know she is the right one for what you want? How do you know you will be in a safe situation? What is the location? Is there sex involved? How do you pay? These questions need to be answered in order for it to be a satisfying session for both of you.

Going to See a Professional Dominatrix

We have all seen the ads in the back of weekly papers or on the Internet offering everything from "Exotic commanding Domina requires you to acquiesce and shower her with perpetual devotion" to "Strap-on play/Greek/No RUSH—$80/hr." Some exclusive pro Dominas are available only through word of mouth; others have entire dungeons and slave retreats devoted to their business. Which one to pick? I recommend calling a variety of them and asking initial questions such as:

- ✔ I am new to this: what can I expect?
- ✔ How long will a session last?
- ✔ What safety precautions will you take if I want to push my limits?
- ✔ What type of equipment do you have?

There is a certain level of professionalism you should expect from a pro Dominatrix. Ideally she will treat you much the same as your hairdresser, mechanic or accountant would, only in leather and heels! These professionals are there to provide a professional service to the best of their ability, so that you leave feeling satisfied and will return. You can spend an hour with the "Strap-on play/Greek/No RUSH—$80/hr" Mistress who is working out of her apartment or you can visit someone who has impeccable standards that she holds herself to in regard to client conduct, safety, and furthering her own craft through education. The choice is yours, but remember: you are going to get what you pay for. Are your fantasies or desires worth playing in a low-end ballpark on the cheap side of town with a bent chain-link fence around the diamond, or are your fantasies worth an exquisite five-star hotel experience? Only you can determine what your comfort level and sexuality is worth.

Vanilla: Everyday life/people/events.

Waxing: Using hot candle wax on another person. It is recommended you find cheap, low-temperature candles when you initially engage in this form of play.

> There is such an enormous amount of pressure on a man to always be in control of himself and others that it's sometimes desirable for him to be able to relinquish power to a woman. Everything else is embellishment on this principle. If the woman is attractive and sadistic, it enhances her power over him. Many men are "afraid" their partners wouldn't understand or appreciate their desire to submit to a woman and indeed, many women are invested in the notion of their strong, commanding partners and would be threatened by the idea of taking control themselves. In my role as a professional Dominant, I initially conduct a phone interview with the people who contact me to determine if we have shared interests. If there is enough common ground, I invite them to make an appointment and book time in my local dungeon. I take care to apply my makeup in a deliberate way that lets the man know that this is a special time. When they are inside and the arrangements have been finalized, I require them to strip off their clothing. Their nakedness and my protected state of being fully clothed adds to the power imbalance they desire.
>
> —The Maestra, professional Dominatrix

The majority of professional Dominas that take their craft seriously will have a website and will clearly post their rules as to what is and what is not acceptable. You must know that if you are going to see a professional Domina, you should not be asking for nor expecting sex. That is typically outside the realm of possibility; even asking for it will get you hung up on or your email ignored. If you want to go see an escort then book an escort; don't expect a professional Domina to provide you with that service.

Whipping Post: A firm upright post with a hook at the top to affix a bottom's wrist cuffs to so he is stretched up and out while he is being whipped or flogged.

> I like to start off with a few simple questions that can give both of us direction:
>
> 1) Tell me three things that you like to do, or are visually attracted too? 2) What is something you consider a gray area? Meaning something you may want to work toward, but currently find a little scary. 3) What do you definitely NOT want to do? I consider this the "Red area" that should never be pushed. Limits must be respected and that is why I work hard to establish strong communication. Even under short time constraints I find that a fun and enjoyable scene can be achieved as long as you maintain and respect boundaries.
>
> —Mistress Jezebel Fatale, professional Dominatrix

Some other questions you can expect to be asked include, "Do you have any health issues I should know about?" and "What would you like to explore when we have time together?" They understand that if you are a newbie, you will be nervous, and the mark of an excellent Domina will be that she can put you at ease on the phone and tease out of you what it is you desire even if you are unsure of it yourself. You don't have to be specific right off the bat. If it is your first time, you can say something as simple as, "I would respectfully like a general overview session that explores many different sensations as I am new and not exactly sure what I really like just yet." That statement will help them prepare because it lets them know your experience level, gives them a starting point to prepare a nice introductory scene, and lets them understand that they won't be pushing your limits too hard.

Gags can be complex and delicious pieces of full head gear. This one has an attachment point at the top to keep submissives where you want them.

Getting into It

Typically, you can book as long an amount of time as you can afford with a professional Domina. In this case, time IS actually money. An average introductory session might be an hour or an hour and a half. After you gain experience and develop a professional relationship with that person, a session might extend to several hours or even days. I know of some pro Dominas that will even travel with a submissive depending on the dynamic of the relationship. Some people are born negotiators and see a professional Domina as just another professional to negotiate with for services to be rendered. Be forewarned that this is not the case in the realm of professional Dominas. They have set their rates according to their skill level, studio space, and equipment. Do you really want to dicker on a price point before you are all tied up and she is about to drip candle wax on your genitals? All you will do is piss her off and not in a good way. If her services are outside of your budget, tell her so and she might be willing to arrange a shorter time period for you.

Once You Get There

Be clean, freshly showered and dressed nicely. Be polite and allow her to start the scene by setting the tone with instructions for you. She is the professional after all, and she will set the tone according to what you discussed on the phone. You should have already discussed your interests and scene preference long before you get to the dungeon. Some states have different laws concerning the exchange of money between consenting adults. Dominas typically charge for what they call the "studio fee"; whatever else you discussed on the phone is between consenting adults outside of that fee. The law is different in each country and sometimes even varying among states in the same country. Before you book your first visit, acquaint yourself with your local laws regarding professional services from a provider such as a Dominatrix. Granted no sex takes place and that is a saving grace, but you will need to educate yourself as to how each locale delineates its sex worker laws, either online or by outright asking the Domina about the boundaries and laws regarding her profession before you arrive for your session. Some professional dungeons will expect you to pay the booking agent and not the Domina, while others will want you to pay them with the cash in an envelope, and no, you can't pay by personal check, but there are some dungeons that will accept credit cards or online payment options such as PayPal. One way or another, you can expect to pay once you arrive, before you use the facilities. Ask about the payment method and rate on the phone when you book your session. If you are annoying, disrespectful, or even try to rip off a pro Domina you will find yourself blacklisted quite quickly in the community. All the pro Dominas talk to each other and word travels very fast among them.

When Visiting a Professional Domina

- ✔ Plays safe. A good professional Dominatrix will respect any of your health issues or limitations, whether emotional, mental or physical. The studio will be clean and hygienic.
- ✔ She will respect and honor your boundaries.
- ✔ She will have a certain amount of empathy regardless of the professional business face that is on the surface. A good Domina needs to have the ability to identify and understand the experiences you are going through and how and when to push you and when to relax.

Once you have begun the scene, you might find that what you had discussed on the phone, such as "I think I want to be tied up," isn't really working for you. Sometimes there is a disconnect between fantasy and the reality of what is actually happening. Don't be shy in expressing this in a respectful way to the Domina. A simple "Excuse me Mistress, but if you don't mind I would like to raise a point: while I initially thought I wanted to be tied up with rope, I find that the rope chafes too much and is hurting me. Would it be possible that we could try some other way of binding me, perhaps the cuffs?" (If this scenario involves your being gagged, you'll need to drop the keys or make whatever nonverbal signal was prearranged.) Any respectable professional will realize that this is not an outlandish request and will be happy to accommodate you, even if her "game face" is stern and demanding. She wants you to have a good time and be satisfied so that you might become a repeat client and as a professional she wants to satisfy her clients. However, don't be so disrespectful as to suddenly change your mind about the boundaries the two of you previously set once in the scene and become demanding, *e.g.,* "Instead of wrapping me in plastic wrap, I want you to stick needles in my cock and balls and then whip the bottoms of my feet!" The first example deals with a variation of a specific activity, while the second example involves two completely different activities that have different boundaries and safety issues associated with them. Boundaries are important and so are manners; you will get much better service if you are polite, respectful and honest.

WIITWD: An acronym for "What It Is That We Do" that is a broad reference to all kinky activities.

After the Session

Be polite and respectful. Many Dominas encourage feedback as to what you felt was positive and what you felt you would like to explore next. If you are not happy with how things went, address your issues in a polite and professional way. (See chapter 4 for more about negotiating.) Sometimes things may not go as you had envisioned and giving them feedback will help them understand how they can sharpen their focus for the next time you book with them. One professional Domina I know takes the time after a scene to ask the submissive to fill out an online questionnaire about the scene the day after and email it to her. She finds that after they have come down out of subspace and can clearly think again, her clients can offer constructive criticism or focus on the positive aspects of what did and didn't work for them in the scene. She uses this method to better understand her clients' needs and wants, and thus can better tailor and sharpen the focus of the next session.

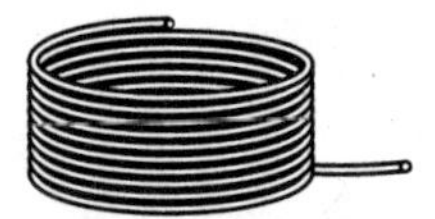

More Things to Think about When Hiring a Professional

- ✔ She must have excellent communication skills, not just verbal but also the ability to read body language, signs and signals.
- ✔ She must have patience, creativity, and the ability to deal immediately with a high-pressure situation that requires cool, clear thinking to resolve.

Going to See a Pro with a Partner

This is a great way to introduce a new partner to enjoying some of the things you do! I highly recommend that more couples go to see a professional Domina as she can share her vast knowledge and expertise in assisting them with their own BDSM dynamic. Professional Dominas often have years of experience and are great at facilitating a couple's fantasies and helping them to discover new things about themselves and new sensations they might enjoy. Sometimes when I am just starting out with a new play partner I will bring her to a pro Domina friend of mine so she can expand the submissive's chain of experiences. Each Domina is like a different artist with varying brushes and colors, painting across the canvas of another's sexuality. I find that she will touch and explore with the person I have brought to her in completely different ways than I will. For a couple that is just starting to explore, this can be a revealing and bonding moment in which they can learn more about each other's sexual desires from a different perspective.

Things That Can Go Wrong and How to Deal with Them

You have talked on the phone and exchanged emails, and are off to see your first professional Domina. You get there and unlike the professional looking space you viewed on the webpage, the studio looks dirty and rundown, or maybe even the Domina isn't as she portrayed herself to be, or perhaps you don't even feel you are safe. You are under no obligation to enter through that door and begin regardless of what you had agreed upon. If someone misrepresents herself or her service you can respectfully say, "I am sorry but I am not comfortable. I think I should go now." If the individual tries to coerce you into paying a cancellation fee or threatens you in any way, pay the fifty dollars and take your leave and then let it be known among your own people that you had a very bad experience and would not recommend her services. There are online boards dedicated to reviewing professional Dominas; a simple online search will reveal them. You can post either a negative or positive review there and search out other reviews of different Dominas. Respected, experienced, professional Dominas take care of themselves and their business, and conduct themselves accordingly.

Zipper: Many clothespins tied along a long cord and then pulled off quickly or slowly depending on how sadistic one is.

Loyalty

Just as you would with any other professional service, you may have to try a number of Dominas to find the dynamic, setting, and personality you like and enjoy exploring. Professional Dominas will hope you'll want to return for a repeat session, but they also know that each one of them offers a varying and unique experience. Some may be experts in feminization and cross-dressing, others might have the advantage in corporal punishment. If what you find with one doesn't work as well as you would like, then you will try another. That's the nature of the service industry, whether you are taking your car to have its oil changed or having your taxes prepared. Typically, newbies looking only for professional Dominas will try three to six different individuals before starting to settle into a professional relationship with one or two of them that offers exactly what they want. Pro Dominas know all this and will not feel hurt or betrayed if you move on; it is the nature of the industry.

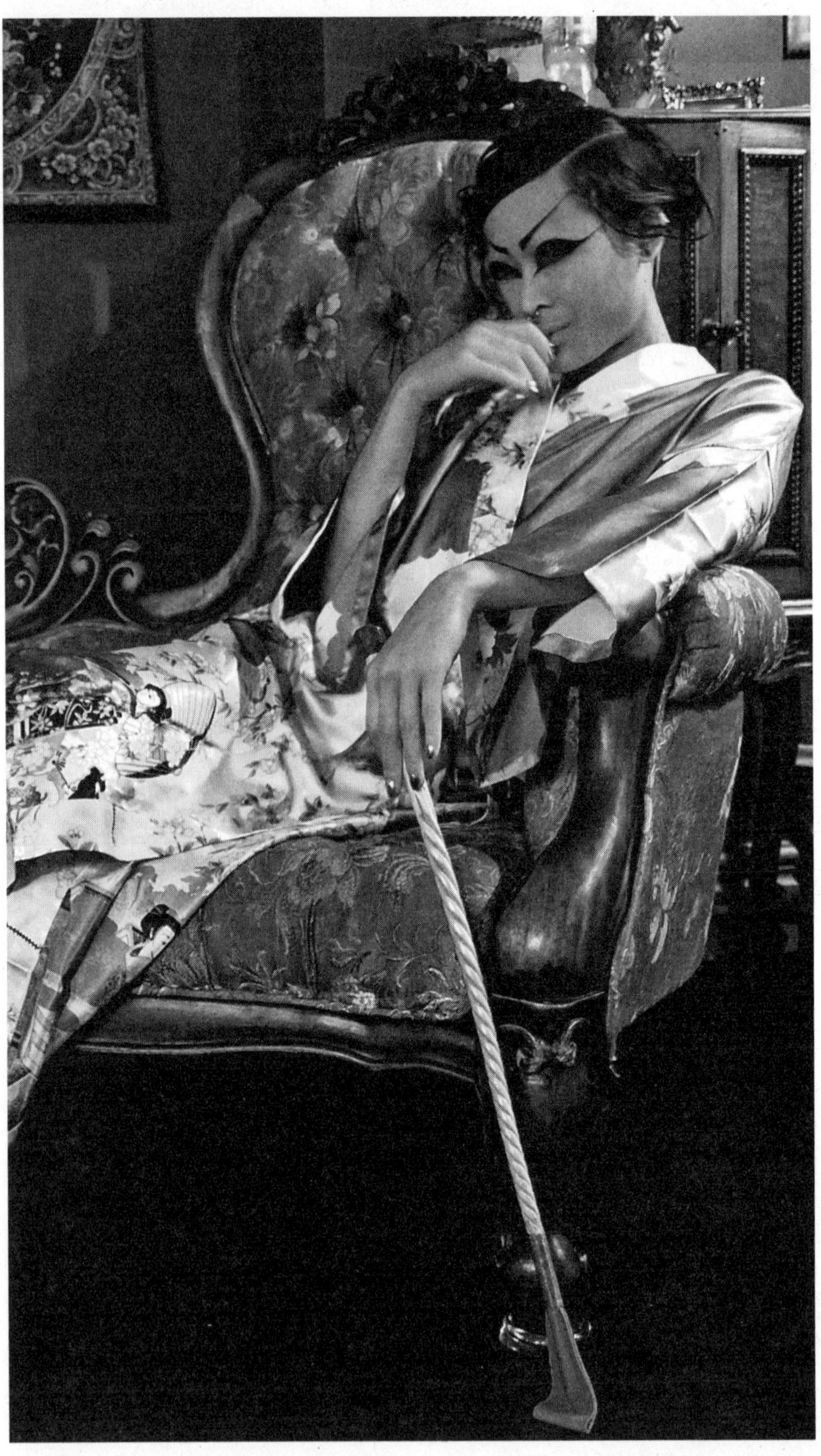

Resources

Further Reading

- *The Better Built Bondage Book: A Complete Guide to Making Your Own Sex Toys, Furniture and BDSM Equipment* by Douglas Kent
- *Bound to Be fFree* by Charles Moster and JJ Madeson
- *The Bride Wore Black Leather…And He Looked Fabulous! An Etiquette Guide for the Rest of Us* by Drew Campbell
- *Erotic Bondage Handbook*, Jay Wiseman
- *Erotic Surrender: The Sensual Joys of Female Submission* by Claudia Varrin
- *The Master's Manual: A Handbook of Erotic Dominance* by Jack Rinella
- *Miss Abernathy's Concise Slave Training Manual* by Christine Abernathy
- *The Mistress Manual: The Good Girl's Guide to Female Dominance* by Lorelei
- *On the Safe Edge: A Manual for SM Play* by Trevor Jacques

- ✔ *Screw the Roses, Send Me the Thorns* by Phillip Miller and Molly Devon
- ✔ *The Seductive Art of Japanese Bondage* by Midori
- ✔ *SM 101* by Jay Wiseman
- ✔ *Two Knotty Boys Showing You the Ropes* by Dan and JD, the Two Knotty Boys

Websites and More

The Internet and magazines are wonderful places to find resources in helping you along in your journey of exploration with kinky sex. Those I have compiled below are just a fraction of the resources out there, but they are ones I personally know of and feel have a wonderful product or service. Online groups are too numerous to list, but many are run by dedicated individuals and there are sure to be some in your local area. Googling will help you find local munches and fetish nights near you. I have met many wonderful toy makers and artistans of kinky toys in my travels and speaking from personal experience those listed below are some of my favorites—but I am always discovering new vendors!

Rope

I exclusively use two makers for all of my rope for teaching and personal use:

Handmade Rope: www.handmaderope.com

Gargoyle Toes Rope: www.gargoyletoes.com

Other Great Rope Makers and Suppliers

Twisted Monk: www.twistedmonk.com

Kinky Ropes: www.kinkyropes.com

Madam Butterfly: www.butterflyrope.com

Clothing and Toys

Northbound Leather: www.northboundleather.com

Come As You Are: www.comeasyouare.com

Master Andre: www.masterandre.com

Priape: www.priape.com

Floggers: www.kaosfloggers.com

Venus Envy (Halifax and Ottawa): www.venusenvy.ca

Fetish jewelry: www.fetjeweller.com

Corsets: www.fittobetied.ca

Whips: www.masterwhipmaker.com

Libido toys: www.libidolondon.com

Aslan Leather: www.aslanleather.com

Ego Assassin Latex Designs: www.ego-assassin.com

The Wild Side Cross Dressing: www.wildside.org

The Stockroom: www.stockroom.com

Deviant and Sinister: www.deviantandsinister.com

Mr. S. Leather: www.mr-s-leather.com

Extreme Restraints: www.extremerestraints.com

BDSM Bed and Breakfasts

Ontario: www.chateausauble.ca

Toronto: www.bentinn.com

British Columbia: www.ravensretreat.com

Seattle: www.mybdsm.com/pages/GypsyArms/seascene.htm

Online and Print Magazines

Eros: www.eros-zine.com

Domination Directory International: www.ddimag.com

Skin Two: www.skintwo.co.uk

Kinky wiki :www.en.smiki.org

Marquis: www.marquis.de

Secret: www.secretmag.com

Bookstores

Outwrite Books (Atlanta): www.outwritebooks.com

This Ain't the Rosedale Library (Toronto): www.thisaint.ca

Come As You Are (Toronto): www.comeasyouare.com

Hot Kink-Related Online Sites

Mine: www.lordmorpheous.com
Maxine X: www.maxinex.com
Artemis Hunter: www.artemishunter.com
Monika Maple: www.monikamaple.com
Orabella: www.kinkyorabella.com
Kink.com: www.kink.com
Chanta Rose: www.chantasbitches.com
Midori: www.planetmidori.com

Educational/ Conferences and Advocacy Groups

U.S.

National Coalition of Sexual Freedom (San Francisco): www.ncsfreedom.org
Leather Leadership Conference (San Francisco): www.leatherleadership.org
Southplains Leather Fest (Dallas): www.southplainsleatherfest.com
Thunder in the Mountains (Colorado): www.thunderinthemountains.com
TES (NYC): www.tes.org
IML (Chicago): www.imrl.com
Black Rose (Maryland): www.br.org
N.O.B.L.E. (New Orleans): www.lanoble.org
Shibaricon (Chicago): www.shibaricon.com
BDSM Events (world listing): www.bdsm-events.com
Knot Guilty (Atlanta): www.knotguilty.org
St.Louis: www.STL3.com
C.L.A.W. (Cleveland): www.clawinfo.org
Mid Atlantic Leather (Washington D.C.): www.leatherweekend.com

Canada

Lupercalia (Edmonton, Canada): www.lupercalia-edmonton.com
Black and Blue Ball (Winnepeg): www.blackandblueball.ca

MLT(Toronto): www.mrlt.com
Breathless (Ottawa): www.breathlessottawa.com
EHBC (Southern Ontario): www.ehbc.ca
Vancouver Dungeon (with car pooling!):
www.vancouverdungeon.com
Libido (Vancouver): www.libidoevents.com
519 LGBT Community Center (Toronto): www.the519.org

Kinky Furniture Makers

Porte Rouge: www.portrouge.net
Master R: www.masterrsdungeons.com

Dating and Online BDSM sites:

Collar Me: www.collarme.com
Bondage: www.bondage.com
ALT: www.alt.com

Museums and Archives

Amsterdam Sex Museum: www.sexmuseumamsterdam.nl
NYC Sex Museum: www.museumofsex.com
Leather Archives and Museum (Chicago):
www.leatherarchives.org

Sex Worker and Other Resources

Toronto

Maggies: www.maggiestoronto.ca
Sex Professionals of Canada: www.spoc.ca/index.html
AIDS Committee of Toronto: www.actoronto.org

Montreal

Stella: www.chezstella.org

San Francisco

Health Resources: www.bayswan.org

New York

Spread Magazine: www.spreadmagazine.org
Sex Workers Project: www.sexworkersproject.org/

Acknowledgments

This book grew out of my experiences as a sex educator and the people, places and events I have encountered in my travels across Canada, the United States, Central America, and Europe while teaching, photographing, and meeting others who are curious about exploring the fascinating subject of human sexuality. I've observed other kinky individuals at play from the SMArt Café in Vienna, where rubber-sheathed patrons nosh off a table atop a cage in which their partners are shackled and bound at their feet, to the sexy byways of Rome and Palermo where women in high heels negotiate the cobblestone streets in a way that would make a goat envious, exhibiting that very sexy and empowered Italian woman's sashay, to the world's largest single night fetish event hosted by Northbound Leather in Toronto, which brings together four thousand like-minded people from around the world, to kinky late-night adventures in minivans with Atlanta soccer moms, to kinky adventures in the private jungle gardens of Costa Rica. What constantly amazes me in meeting people around the world is how kinky we are regardless of race, language, culture or social status. As humans, our capacity for kinky sex and curiosity seems to be ingrained. Sex should be a loving act, but it can also be very primal at times, and aggressive and passive, sometimes at the same time. I find myself eternally curious about how we as sexual beings constantly negotiate toward mutual enjoyment.

This book has come about in an attempt to demystify a subject that is routinely portrayed by the media in an unfavorable, sensational light. I want to encourage others to explore their sexuality in a safe way without fear of reprisal, guilt, or shame either with one partner, or several, or solo. Flirt with your urges and explore. Take your time to learn about what gets you hot and bothered and rest assured that just because you like a little bit of "tie me up with some slap and tickle" in the bedroom doesn't necessarily mean you will give up your day job and start wearing leather 24/7. Being a well-rounded person and letting your sexuality complement your life is the goal. As with most things in life, balance is essential. Occasionally I see newbies immerse themselves in the community with such vigor and excitement they let the other aspects of their lives lapse and I always caution against that. Maintaining balance is essential. For instance, I enjoy scuba diving just as much, albeit differently, as I do going to a fetish event and binding beautiful partners and setting their nerves alight, although both of these activities involve wearing lots of rubber.

Writing this book has been a wonderful learning experience for me. The concept of writing a book being like giving birth held true—except no one warned me about the corners!

My thanks go to my editor, Kevin, who helped put the polish on my words; the Cundari Agency for seeing raw talent and encouraging it—and for the chicken wings; Midori for her hard work at seeding the way for many of us and for her encouragement over the years; kharma, who has stalwartly stood by me all these years despite my teasing; Come As You Are for their support as I developed my teaching career; Northbound Leather for all of their support and delicious toys; Rob and The Bobbyfive Gallery crew; The Rhino Bar and Grill, my home away from home on Queen Street West in Toronto where I would inevitably wind up banging away on my laptop for hours on winter nights; Effi and gregg whose hard work let me put together my events and have them come off as effortless; Joe, for his mentorship; Darren and Geordie for their web expertise; Michelle and Joey for all their help in my early development as a photographer; Byrd, doll, Peter, Tracy, Tim and Vanessa for all of their support and harbor; Craiger for his amazing parties; Delano for all the great visits and long nighttime discussions on kink, photography, and pop culture during my sojourns in New York; the individuals who shared their stories in this book, all true and as varied as my friends; my beautiful models who grace these pages; Dart and Artemis for asking intriguing questions; and all those I have touched lives with in my travels.

About the Author

Morpheous (B.Ed) is a Toronto-based author and sex educator who has taught workshops and lectured for sexuality groups and universities across North America and Europe for the past decade. He believes people can enhance their sex lives through mutual exploration and trust. Visit him at: www.lordmorpheous.com and then write him something interesting.